# Cucumber Cookbook

Over 35 hands-on recipes to efficiently master the art
of behaviour-driven development using Cucumber-JVM

**Shankar Garg**

BIRMINGHAM - MUMBAI

# Cucumber Cookbook

First published: May 2015

Production reference: 1260515

Published by Packt Publishing Ltd.
Livery Place
35 Livery Street
Birmingham B3 2PB, UK.

ISBN 978-1-78528-600-1

www.packtpub.com

# Credits

**Author**
Shankar Garg

**Reviewers**
John Kamenik
Nguyen Quang Phuong
Abhishek Yadav

**Commissioning Editor**
Priya Singh

**Acquisition Editor**
Larissa Pinto

**Content Development Editor**
Sriram Neelakantan

**Technical Editors**
Namrata Patil
Bharat Patil

**Copy Editors**
Puja Lalwani
Laxmi Subramanian

**Project Coordinator**
Vijay Kushlani

**Proofreaders**
Stephen Copestake
Safis Editing

**Indexer**
Rekha Nair

**Graphics**
Jason Monteiro

**Production Coordinator**
Melwyn D'sa

**Cover Work**
Melwyn D'sa

# About the Author

**Shankar Garg** is an Agile enthusiast with expertise in automation testing. Currently, he is working as a senior consultant, testing with Xebia IT Architects, India.

He started as a Java developer but his love for breaking things got him into testing. He has worked on the automation of many projects for web, mobile, and SOA technologies. Right now, he is in love with Cucumber, Selenium, Appium, and Groovy.

Prior to working with Xebia, he worked for Jabong.com, Honeywell, and Tata Consultancy Services (TCS).

He is a Certified Scrum Master (CSM), Certified Tester (ISTQB), Certified Programmer for Java (SCJP 5.0) and Oracle 9i (OCA).

I would like to thank my family, especially my wife and daughter, for putting up with my late night / early morning writing sessions. Without your support, this book would not have been possible. Thanks for your patience and understanding.

I would also like to thank Xebia IT Architects, India, because if it were not for the inspiration that I got in Xebia IT Architects, India, I would have never thought of writing a book, let alone finishing it on time. All credit goes to the Xebia DNA. Thank you, Xebia!!

# About the Reviewers

**Nguyen Quang Phuong** works at a small start-up company, Mobilus (http://mobilus. co.jp). Mobilus provides a real-time communication platform and an SDK called Konnect. All members are working hard to create more innovative products.

As a full-stack engineer, he works from the frontend to the backend. In the frontend, he has experiences working with iOS applications and responsive, real-time web services for mobile browser and PC browsers. He also works on advanced frameworks such as Meteor to create an application that runs everywhere (browser, iOS, and Android-native applications) with JavaScript or HTML5. In the backend, he designs APIs and data models and does server tasks, such as hosting environments.

He is also a member of the Meteor community and takes part in a project to translate Discover Meteor into Vietnamese (http://vi.discovermeteor.com/). In this project, he learned how to make real-time applications with JavaScript.

I want to thank my colleague Takeharu Oshida, who teaches me a lot about new technologies and who introduced this book to me.

**Abhishek Yadav** is an experienced consultant having expertise in automation testing, including automation framework development. Currently, he is working with Xebia IT Architects India Pvt. Ltd., Gurgaon.

He has primarily worked on Selenium WebDriver and Java. Apart from this, he also has expertise in Cucumber, JMeter, AutoIt, Maven, TestNG, and Appium. Other than testing, he has a good exposure of technologies such as HTML, CSS, JQuery, JavaScript, and SQL.

He shares his automation experience through his blog Hello Selenium (`http://www.helloselenium.com`). These experiences have helped him a lot in reviewing this book. He has also taken help from his colleagues, wherever required, to make this book more informative to the readers.

# www.PacktPub.com

## Support files, eBooks, discount offers, and more

For support files and downloads related to your book, please visit www.PacktPub.com.

Did you know that Packt offers eBook versions of every book published, with PDF and ePub files available? You can upgrade to the eBook version at www.PacktPub.com and as a print book customer, you are entitled to a discount on the eBook copy. Get in touch with us at service@packtpub.com for more details.

At www.PacktPub.com, you can also read a collection of free technical articles, sign up for a range of free newsletters and receive exclusive discounts and offers on Packt books and eBooks.

https://www2.packtpub.com/books/subscription/packtlib

Do you need instant solutions to your IT questions? PacktLib is Packt's online digital book library. Here, you can search, access, and read Packt's entire library of books.

## Why Subscribe?

- ▸ Fully searchable across every book published by Packt
- ▸ Copy and paste, print, and bookmark content
- ▸ On demand and accessible via a web browser

## Free Access for Packt account holders

If you have an account with Packt at www.PacktPub.com, you can use this to access PacktLib today and view 9 entirely free books. Simply use your login credentials for immediate access.

*I dedicate this book to my mother, whom I lost to Amyotrophic lateral sclerosis (ALS) disease while I was writing this book. We were really close and watching her die everyday was not easy at all. However, I was really motivated by her desire to live even when in so much pain and agony. All she wanted in life for me was to be happy. I really want to thank her for all the love, affection, and care.*

*In the end, I want to say that I really love you mother and will always miss you. You will always be alive in my memories.*

# Table of Contents

# Preface

Cucumber JVM is one of the fastest-growing tools that offer a cutting-edge platform to conceptualize and implement behaviour-driven development (BDD). The variety of features available within Cucumber bolsters and enhances experiences of implementing BDD for both business and development teams.

This cookbook has around 40 recipes. It takes you on a learning journey, where you start from basic concepts such as Feature files, Step Definitions, and then moves on to advanced concepts such as Hooks, Tags, configuration, and integration with Jenkins and test automation frameworks. Each chapter has multiple recipes, with the first recipe introducing the main concept of that chapter; the complexity level of each recipe increases as you progress through the chapter. The book has sufficient topics for product owners, business analysts, testers, developers, and everyone who wants to implement BDD.

This book is written with an assumption that the reader already has some idea about Cucumber. If you are new to Cucumber, it is advisable to go over my blog first:

- **Blog 1**: *How to integrate Eclipse with Cucumber plugin* `https://shankargarg. wordpress.com/2015/04/26/how-to-integrate-eclipse-with- cucumber-plugin/`
- **Blog 2**: *Create a Cucumber Project by Integrating Maven-Cucumber-Selenium-Eclipse* `https://shankargarg.wordpress.com/2015/04/29/create-a-cucumber- project-by-integrating-maven-cucumber-selenium-eclipse/`

These two blogs will help you integrate Cucumber and Eclipse and help you create and run a basic project.

All of the code explained in this book is committed on GitHub. Here is the URL of the code repository: `https://github.com/ShankarGarg/CucumberBook.git`.

This repository has five projects:

 ▸ **Cucumber-book-blog**: This project is used in the blogs mentioned earlier to start with Cucumber, Maven, and Eclipse

 ▸ **CucumberCookbook**: This project is used in chapters 1 to 5

 ▸ **CucumberWebAutomation, CucumberMobileAutomation, and CucumberRESTAutomation**: This project is used in *Chapter 6, Building Cucumber Frameworks*

# What this book covers

*Chapter 1, Writing Feature Files*, covers unique aspect of Cucumber – the Gherkin language and usage of Gherkin language to write meaningful and smart Feature files. This chapter will also cover different keywords, such as files Scenario, Steps, Scenario Outlines, and Data Tables.

*Chapter 2, Creating Step Definitions*, covers basic concepts and usage of Glue Code/Step Definitions, and regular expressions to come up with efficient and optimized Step Definitions. This chapter will also elaborate the concept of String and Data Table transformations.

*Chapter 3, Enabling Fixtures*, covers the advanced concepts of implementing fixtures by Tags and Hooks. Here not only the individual concepts of Tags and Hooks are explained, but practical example of using Tags and Hooks combination is also explained.

*Chapter 4, Configuring Cucumber*, deals with integration of Cucumber with JUnit and the concept of Cucumber Options. Here you will learn various practical examples of using Cucumber Options and different types of reports that can be generated with Cucumber.

*Chapter 5, Running Cucumber*, covers topics of running Cucumber from the Terminal and from Jenkins. You will learn Cucumber integration with Jenkins and GitHub to implement **Continuous Integration and Continuous Deployment** (**CICD**) pipelines. Then you will learn parallel execution to take full advantage of Cucumber.

*Chapter 6, Building Cucumber Frameworks*, covers detailed Steps to create robust test automation frameworks to automate web applications, mobile applications, and REST services.

# What you need for this book

Before starting with Cucumber, let's make sure that we have all the necessary software installed.

The pre-requisites for Cucumber are as follows:

- Java (Version 7 or later) as the programming language
- Eclipse as the IDE
- Maven as the build tool
- Firefox as the Browser
- The Eclipse-Maven plugin
- The Eclipse-Cucumber plugin
- Jenkins
- GIT
- Appium
- Android SDK

# Who this book is for

This book is intended for business and development personnel who want to use Cucumber for behavior-driven development and test automation. Readers with some familiarity with Cucumber will find this book of most benefit.

Since the main objective of this book is to create test automation frameworks, previous experience in automation will be helpful.

# Sections

In this book, you will find several headings that appear frequently (Getting ready, How to do it, How it works, There's more, and See also).

To give clear instructions on how to complete a recipe, we use these sections as follows:

## Getting ready

This section tells you what to expect in the recipe, and describes how to set up any software or any preliminary settings required for the recipe.

## How to do it...

This section contains the steps required to follow the recipe.

## How it works...

This section usually consists of a detailed explanation of what happened in the previous section.

## There's more...

This section consists of additional information about the recipe in order to make the reader more knowledgeable about the recipe.

## See also

This section provides helpful links to other useful information for the recipe.

# Conventions

In this book, you will find a number of text styles that distinguish between different kinds of information. Here are some examples of these styles and an explanation of their meaning.

Code words in text, database table names, folder names, filenames, file extensions, pathnames, dummy URLs, user input, and Twitter handles are shown as follows: "We can include other contexts through the use of the `include` directive."

A block of code is set as follows:

```
@When("^user enters \"(.*?)\" in username field$")
  public void user_enters_in_username_field(String userName) {
     //print the value of data passed from Feature file
     System.out.println(userName);
  }
```

When we wish to draw your attention to a particular part of a code block, the relevant lines or items are set in bold:

```
Scenario: checking pre-condition, action and results
   Given user is on Application landing page
   When user clicks Sign in button
   Then user is on login screen
```

Any command-line input or output is written as follows:

```
mvn test -Dcucumber.options="--tags @sanity"
```

**New terms** and **important words** are shown in bold. Words that you see on the screen, for example, in menus or dialog boxes, appear in the text like this: "Click on the timestamp on the build. And then click on **Console Output**."

 Warnings or important notes appear in a box like this.

 Tips and tricks appear like this.

# Reader feedback

Feedback from our readers is always welcome. Let us know what you think about this book—what you liked or disliked. Reader feedback is important for us as it helps us develop titles that you will really get the most out of.

To send us general feedback, simply e-mail feedback@packtpub.com, and mention the book's title in the subject of your message.

If there is a topic that you have expertise in and you are interested in either writing or contributing to a book, see our author guide at www.packtpub.com/authors.

# Customer support

Now that you are the proud owner of a Packt book, we have a number of things to help you to get the most from your purchase.

## Downloading the example code

You can download the example code files from your account at http://www.packtpub.com for all the Packt Publishing books you have purchased. If you purchased this book elsewhere, you can visit http://www.packtpub.com/support and register to have the files e-mailed directly to you.

## Errata

Although we have taken every care to ensure the accuracy of our content, mistakes do happen. If you find a mistake in one of our books—maybe a mistake in the text or the code—we would be grateful if you could report this to us. By doing so, you can save other readers from frustration and help us improve subsequent versions of this book. If you find any errata, please report them by visiting `http://www.packtpub.com/submit-errata`, selecting your book, clicking on the **Errata Submission Form** link, and entering the details of your errata. Once your errata are verified, your submission will be accepted and the errata will be uploaded to our website or added to any list of existing errata under the Errata section of that title.

To view the previously submitted errata, go to `https://www.packtpub.com/books/content/support` and enter the name of the book in the search field. The required information will appear under the **Errata** section.

## Piracy

Piracy of copyrighted material on the Internet is an ongoing problem across all media. At Packt, we take the protection of our copyright and licenses very seriously. If you come across any illegal copies of our works in any form on the Internet, please provide us with the location address or website name immediately so that we can pursue a remedy.

Please contact us at `copyright@packtpub.com` with a link to the suspected pirated material.

We appreciate your help in protecting our authors and our ability to bring you valuable content.

## Questions

If you have a problem with any aspect of this book, you can contact us at `questions@packtpub.com`, and we will do our best to address the problem.

# 1

# Writing Feature Files

In this chapter, we will cover the following topics:

- ▶ Writing your first Feature file with one Scenario
- ▶ Creating Scenarios with different Steps
- ▶ Creating a Scenario with the And and But keywords
- ▶ Writing a Feature file with multiple Scenarios
- ▶ Adding Background to Feature files
- ▶ Sending multiple arguments in Steps
- ▶ Using complex data types to store data
- ▶ Implementing Scenario Outlines
- ▶ Creating a Feature file in a language other than English
- ▶ Combining Scenarios, Background, and Scenario Outlines

## Introduction

In Cucumber Framework, business requirements are specified in Feature files, which are written in the Gherkin Language. So it becomes very important for us to understand the power and usage of the Gherkin language to come up with efficient and optimized Feature files.

This chapter will cover the usage of the Gherkin language to write meaningful and smart Feature files. We will start with some simple recipes to create a Feature file with one Scenario and will gradually move to recipes that are more complex where we create Feature files with multiple Scenarios, Backgrounds, and Scenario Outlines. We will also cover concepts and keywords, such as Feature, Scenario, Steps, Background, Scenario Outline and Data Tables.

In this chapter, we will only focus on Feature files. Step Definitions and automation libraries will be covered in later chapters. Initially, you may not understand everything about the concepts in this chapter, but things will become clearer as you read on.

# Writing your first Feature file with one Scenario

Let's assume you are a **Product Owner** (**PO**) or a **Business Analyst** (**BA**). Your team is creating a web application and you need to write specifications for that application. A very simple and basic specification for that web application is when we enter the URL of that application in a browser, the application should load. So how do we write this specification in Cucumber? We will be covering this in this recipe.

## How to do it...

In this recipe, we are going to create a simple Feature file with only one Scenario that tests whether the web page has loaded or not.

Let's create a `page_load.feature` file:

```
Feature: Test Git web Application
In order to Test Git web Application
As a user
I want to specify the application flow

Scenario: Web Site loads
application page load should be quick

Given application URL is ready with the user
When user enters the URL in browser
Then application page loads
```

## How it works...

In Cucumber we write our requirements in plain English like Language, **Gherkin**. Gherkin is a domain-specific language that has a very well-defined syntax. It works on the basis of some predefined **keywords**. In the preceding example, the highlighted portions of the text are Gherkin's keywords and the rest is dependent on the application under test.

Let's understand each keyword in more detail.

## Feature

In Cucumber, Feature files contain business requirements. The text that immediately follows the Feature keyword, and is in the same line, is the Title of the Feature file. Three (optional) Text lines that follow the Feature keyword line are Intent of the Feature file and intent text is whatever we want to write, up until the first Scenario. Feature file should contain either Scenario or Scenario Outline. The naming conventions for Feature files should be lowercase with underscores, for example, `login.feature` and `home_page.feature`. The names of Scenarios and Feature files must be unique.

## Scenarios

Scenarios are like test cases and start with the Scenario keyword in a new line (different from the Feature intent). The text that immediately follows the Scenario keyword, and is on the same line, is the **Scenario Title**. Three (optional) Text lines that follow the Scenario keyword line are **Intent** of the Scenario. All Scenarios perform following:

- ▸ Get the system into a particular state
- ▸ Poke it (perform some action)
- ▸ Examine the new state

## Steps

Scenarios contain Steps which are equivalent to test Steps and use the following keywords to denote them: Given, When, Then, But, and And (case sensitive).

> When you save the Feature files mentioned in this chapter and run them, in the first run, Cucumber is going to give errors for the missing Step Definition files, along with suggestions for Step Definitions. To resolve these errors, copy the suggestions given by Cucumber and paste them into a default Step Definition file.

# Creating Scenarios with different Steps

When we specify a business requirement, we need to specify the pre-conditions, user actions, and expected output. Let's first understand what each of these mean:

- ▸ **Pre-condition**: This sets the **Application Under Test** (**AUT**) in a state where the test case can be executed, or establishing the application context.
- ▸ **User action**: This refers to the action that a user performs that is in line with the Scenario objective.
- ▸ **Expected output**: This refers to the application's response after the user action.

So let's have this specification written in Cucumber in this recipe.

## How to do it...

In this recipe, we are going to update the Feature file we created in the previous recipe by using the keywords `Given`, `When` and `Then`

```
Feature: login Page
  In order to test login page
  As a Registered user
  I want to specify the login conditions

  Scenario: checking pre-condition, action and results
    Given user is on Application landing page
    When user clicks Sign in button
    Then user is on login screen
```

## How it works...

A Cucumber Scenario consists of Steps identified with keywords such as Given, When, Then, And, But, and so on. These have been defined as follows:

- ▶ **Given**: Preconditions are mentioned in the `Given` keyword. The Steps of the Given keyword put the system in to a known state, which is necessary for the user action. Avoid talking about user interaction in Given Steps.

- ▶ **When**: The purpose of the `When` Steps is to describe the user action.

- ▶ **Then**: The purpose of `Then` Steps is to observe the expected output. The observations should be related to the business value/benefit of your Feature description.

# Creating a Scenario with the And and But keywords

When we specify a business requirement, sometimes there are multiple pre-conditions, user actions, and expected outcomes. So how do we write these specifications in Cucumber?

## Getting ready...

Based on what we have learned so far we know how to create Scenarios with one Given, When, and Then keyword. Now, if we need to add multiple **Steps**, then we can update our Feature file like this:

```
Feature: login Page
  In order to test login page
  As a Registered user
  I want to specify the login conditions
```

```
Scenario: without and & but
    Given user is on Application landing page
    Given Sign in button is present on screen
    When user clicks on Sign in button
    Then user can see login screen
    When user enters "ShankarGarg" in username field
    When user enters "123456" in password field
    When user clicks Sign in button
    Then user is on home page
    Then title of home page is "GitHub"
```

The problem here is that the keywords `Given`, `When`, and `Then` are repeated and the readability is thus affected. Having readable Feature files is one of biggest advantages of Cucumber. So how do we maintain the readability of Feature files? Let's figure this out in this recipe.

## How to do it...

In this recipe, we are going to add one more Scenario and will use the `And` and `But` keywords:

```
Feature: login Page
    In order to test login page
    As a Registered user
    I want to specify the login conditions

    Scenario: with and & but
        Given user is on Application landing page
        And Sign in button is present on screen
        When user clicks on Sign in button
        Then user is displayed login screen
        When user enters "ShankarGarg" in username field
        And user enters "123456" in password field
        And user clicks Sign in button
        Then user is on home page
        And title of home page is "GitHub"
        But Sign in button is not present
```

## How it works...

The `And` and `But` keywords will be useful here. These keywords help to increase the expressiveness and readability of the Feature file:

- ▶ **And**: This is used for statements that are an addition to the previous Steps and represent positives statements.

- ▶ **But**: This is used for statements that are an addition to previous Steps and represent negative statements.

In a Step Definitions file, And and But are listed as Given/When/Then, the keyword that they appear after. There are no And and But keywords in Step Definitions.

# Writing a Feature file with multiple Scenarios

Feature files contain possible Scenarios for a particular functionality. This is like writing all possible requirements that a Feature should meet when it is implemented. So let's write these specifications in Cucumber in the following section.

## How to do it...

We will create a new Feature file called `home_page.feature`, which will cover the functionality of the default content of `https://github.com/`, the **Bootcamp** section, and the top banner content. We will create a different Scenario for each functionality. Take a look at the following screenshot for more clarity:

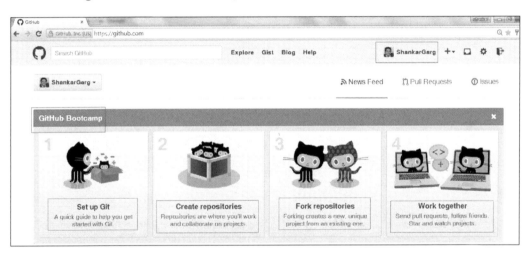

```
Feature: Home Page
  In order to test Home Page of application
  As a Registered user
  I want to specify the features of home page

  Scenario: Home Page Default content
    Given user is on Github home page
    Then user gets a GitHub bootcamp section
    And username is also displayed on right corner
```

```
Scenario: GitHub Bootcamp Section
  Given user is on GitHub home page
  When user focuses on GitHub Bootcamp Section
  Then user gets an option to setup git
  And user gets an option to create repository
  And user gets an option to Fork Repository
  And user gets an option to work together

Scenario: Top Banner content
  Given user is on GitHub home page
  When user focuses on Top Banner
  Then user gets an option of home page
  And user gets an option to search
  And user gets settings options
  And user gets an option to logout
```

## How it works...

A Cucumber Feature file can have any number of Scenarios as required. Some points to keep in mind are as follows:

- One Feature file normally focuses on one functionality of the application, such as login page, home page, and so on.
- One Scenario refers to one sub-Feature of that functionality, such as the new customer page, delete customer page, and so on.

When we have multiple Scenarios in a Feature file, we should always follow the Stateless Scenarios Guideline. Let's understand this guideline better—each Scenario must make sense and should be executed independently of any other Scenario. The result of one Scenario/ Feature should not affect the other Scenario.

These are the benefits of independent Scenarios:

- Feature files are easier and fun to understand
- You can only run a subset of Scenarios, as all the required Steps of a Scenario are mentioned in the Scenario itself
- In comparison to dependent Scenarios, independent Scenarios will be more eligible candidates for *parallel execution*

**Downloading the example code**

You can download the example code files from your account at `http://www.packtpub.com` for all the Packt Publishing books you have purchased. If you purchased this book elsewhere, you can visit `http://www.packtpub.com/support` and register to have the files e-mailed directly to you.

# Adding Backgrounds to Feature files

When we write Feature files, we write multiple Scenarios. Now all of these Scenarios start from one particular point. If I'm writing home page Scenarios, then I need to start the flow from the login functionality. So it is better to write the repetitive Steps at one place rather than in all Scenarios. Let's understand how to do this in the next Section.

## Getting ready

Based on what we have learned so far, this is what our Feature file will look like:

```
Feature: Home Page
  In order to test Home Page of application
  As a Registered user
  I want to specify the features of home page

  Scenario: Home Page Default content
    Given a registered user exists
    Given user is on GitHub login page
    When user enters username
    And user enters password
    And user clicks on login button
    Then user is on Application home page
    And user gets a GitHub bootcamp section

  Scenario: GitHub Bootcamp Section
    Given user is on GitHub loginpage
    When user enters username
    And user enters password
    And user clicks on login button
    Then user is on Application home page
    When user focuses on GitHub Bootcamp Section
    Then user gets an option to setup git

  Scenario: Top Banner content
    Given user is on GitHub login page
    When user enters username
    And user enters password
    And user clicks on login button
    Then user is on Application home page
    When user focuses on Top Banner
    Then user gets a logout option
```

The problem here is that first five statements are repeated in all the Scenarios. This affects the readability of the Feature files, and there is a lot of duplicated effort.

The problems with this way of writing Feature files are:

- ▸ **Repetition**: Many statements are repeated in all the Scenarios
- ▸ **Readability**: The readability of the Feature files is affected.
- ▸ **Duplication**: Copying these Steps to all the Scenarios is redundant.
- ▸ **Maintainability**: Even if a single Step changes, we have to change all occurrences.

## How to do it...

We are going to update the `home_page.feature` file and we are going to use the `Background` keyword to put the common Steps across all the Scenarios in one place:

```
Feature: Home Page
    In order to test Home Page of application
    As a Registered user
    I want to specify the features of home page

    Background: flow till home page
      Given user is on Application home page
      When user enters username
      And user enters password
      And user clicks on login button
      Then user is on Application home page

    Scenario: Home Page Default content
        Then user gets a GitHub bootcamp section

    Scenario: GitHub Bootcamp Section
        When user focuses on GitHub Bootcamp Section
        Then user gets an option to setup git

    Scenario: Top Banner content
        When user focuses on Top Banner
        Then user gets an option of home page
```

## How it works...

Here, we have used the Background keyword. All the Steps mentioned in the Background keyword will be executed before each Scenario or Scenario Outline in a Feature file. Let's understand this keyword in greater detail:

- There can be only one Background in one Feature file and it allows us to set a precondition for all Scenarios in a Feature file.

- A Background is like a Scenario, containing a number of Steps.

- Background is run before each Scenario, but after the **BeforeScenario** Hooks. (We will read about Hooks in *Chapter 3, Enabling Fixtures*).

- The title and multiline description / intent of Background are optional.

- Since the Steps mentioned in Background will be run for all Scenarios in a Feature file, we need to be careful when adding the Steps to Background. For example, we should not add a Step that is not common to all Scenarios.

This is what the output of the preceding file looks like:

```
T E S T S
-----------------------------------------------------------
Running com.CucumberOptions.RunCukeTest
Feature: Home Page
  In order to test Home Page of application
  As a Registered user
  I want to specify the features of home page

  Background: flow till home page              # HomePage.feature:6
    Given user is on Application landing page   # DemoStepsDefinition.user_is_on_Application_landing_page()
    When user enters username                   # DemoStepsDefinition.user_enters_username()
    And user enters password                    # DemoStepsDefinition.user_enters_password()
    And user clicks on login button             # DemoStepsDefinition.user_clicks_on_login_button()
    Then user is on Application home page        # DemoStepsDefinition.user_is_on_Application_home_page()

  Scenario: Home Page Default content            # HomePage.feature:13   Scenario 1 is executed after Background
    Then user gets a github bootcamp section     # DemoStepsDefinition.user_gets_a_github_bootcamp_section()

  Background: flow till home page              # HomePage.feature:6
    Given user is on Application landing page   # DemoStepsDefinition.user_is_on_Application_landing_page()
    When user enters username                   # DemoStepsDefinition.user_enters_username()
    And user enters password                    # DemoStepsDefinition.user_enters_password()
    And user clicks on login button             # DemoStepsDefinition.user_clicks_on_login_button()
    Then user is on Application home page        # DemoStepsDefinition.user_is_on_Application_home_page()

  Scenario: GitHub Bootcamp Section              # HomePage.feature:16   Scenario 2 is executed after Background
    When user focuses on GitHub Bootcamp Section # DemoStepsDefinition.user_focuses_on_GitHub_Bootcamp_Section()
    Then user gets an option to setup git        # DemoStepsDefinition.user_gets_an_option_to_setup_git()

  Background: flow till home page              # HomePage.feature:6
    Given user is on Application landing page   # DemoStepsDefinition.user_is_on_Application_landing_page()
    When user enters username                   # DemoStepsDefinition.user_enters_username()
    And user enters password                    # DemoStepsDefinition.user_enters_password()
    And user clicks on login button             # DemoStepsDefinition.user_clicks_on_login_button()
    Then user is on Application home page        # DemoStepsDefinition.user_is_on_Application_home_page()

  Scenario: Top Banner content                   # HomePage.feature:20   Scenario 3 is executed after Background
    When user focuses on Top Banner              # DemoStepsDefinition.user_focuses_on_Top_Banner()
    Then user gets an option of home page        # DemoStepsDefinition.user_gets_an_option_of_home_page()
```

Don't use `Background` to set up a complicated state unless that state is actually something the client needs to know.

► Keep your `Background` section short because you expect a person to remember these Steps when you are adding a new Scenario

► Make your `Background` section vivid, because that way it will be easier for a person to remember it

# Sending multiple arguments in Steps

When we talk about testing, data-driven testing is a very famous approach. Until now, we have focused on what our Steps intend to do. The questions that now come to mind are as follows:

► Can our Steps also send test data?

► What kind of test data can our Steps send?

► Can we send mixed data types in one single Step?

Put on a BA's shoes and let's write some Scenarios for the GitHub user registration page and login functionality.

## How to do it...

We are going to update the `login.feature` file and add two Scenarios, where we are going to pass arguments in Steps:

```
Feature: login Page
  In order to test login page
  As a Registered user
  I want to specify the login conditions

  Scenario: New User Registration
    Given user is on Application landing page
    When user enters "ShankarGarg" in username field
    And user enters "sgarg@gmail.com" in password field
    And user enters "123456" in password field
    And user clicks on Signup for GitHub button
    Then user is successfully registered

  Scenario: login
    Given user is on Application landing page
    And Sign in button is present on screen
    When user clicks on Sign in button
    Then user is displayed login screen
    When user enters "ShankarGarg" in username field
```

```
And user enters "123456" in password field
And user clicks Sign in button
Then user is on home page
And title of home page is "GitHub"
```

## How it works...

In the preceding Feature file, focus on the text written in " ". This is our test data. The text mentioned in between " " in Steps is associated to Capture groups in Step Definition files.

An example of Step Definition for one of the Steps is:

```
@When("^user enters \"(.*?)\" in username field$")
    public void user_enters_in_username_field(String userName) {
        //print the value of data passed from Feature file
        System.out.println(userName);
    }
```

The output of the preceding `System.out.println` will be `ShankarGarg` (test data that we have passed in the Feature file).

 Now, since you have learned how to pass test data in Steps, try your hand at the following:

▶ Send String and integer data in the same Step.

▶ Send a List in a Step; for example: "Monday, Tuesday, Wednesday".

# Using complex data types to store data

In the previous recipe, we learnt how we can send data in Steps, which can be used by the application for processing. The data that we have sent up to this point has been either Strings or integers. But what if we want to send data structures that are more complex and span across multiple lines?

## Getting ready

Let's write a Scenario for this functionality—we want to verify whether various users exist or not:

```
Scenario: Existing user Verification
    Given user is on Application landing page
    Then we verify user "Shankar" with password "P@ssword123",
phone "999" exists
    Then we verify user "Ram" with password "P@ssword456", phone "
888" exists
```

```
      Then we verify user "Sham" with password "P@ssword789", phone
    "666" exists
```

The problem with this approach of writing Feature files is that Feature files are not expressive enough and there is a lot of repetition.

## How to do it...

We are going to add one more Scenario to the `login.feature` file, and we are going to use Data Table to send a large set of test data along a Step:

```
Scenario: Existing user Verification

Given user is on Application landing page
    Then we verify following user exists
        | name    | email           | phone |
        | Shankar | sgarg@email.com | 999   |
        | Ram     | ram@email.com   | 888   |
        | Sham    | sham@email.org  | 666   |
```

## How it works...

Here we have used Data Tables. Tables as arguments to Steps are handy for specifying larger datasets. Let's understand Data Tables in more detail:

- Tables as arguments to Steps are handy to specify larger datasets.
- The first row of a Data Table is always the header row, where we specify the headers for each column. All the other rows in a Data Table are data rows, which contain the actual data that will be used by the application.
- Data tables will be passed to the Step Definition as the last argument.
- Don't confuse Data Tables with Scenario Outline tables.
- Data tables are very easy to handle in Step Definition files as well. This is what a sample Step Definition code looks like:

```
@Then("^we verify following user exists$")
public void we_verify_following_user_exists(DataTable
userDetails){
   //Write the code to handle Data Table
   List<List<String>> data = userdetails.raw();
   System.out.println(data.get(1).get(1));
}
```

In the preceding code sample, the Data Table has been converted into a List of String and can be handled very easily thereafter.

Data table transformation has been explained in detail in the Transforming Data Tables to parse test data recipe in *Chapter 2, Creating Step Definitions*.

# Implementing Scenario Outlines

In the previous recipe, we learnt how we can send test data in Steps itself, which can be used by the application for processing. Until now, the data was associated with one particular Step (implemented by Data Tables); but what if I want to send data which is related to the whole Scenario, and what if I want to repeat all the Steps of a Scenario again and again for different sets of data? This is a classic case of data-driven testing. This will be implemented by using a Scenario Outline.

## Getting ready

Let's create a Scenario for a login functionality where we want to test all the possible Scenarios where the login will fail. Based on what we have learned so far, this is how our Scenario will look:

```
Scenario: login fail - wrong username
   Given user is on Application landing page
   When user clicks on Sign in button
   Then user is displayed login screen
   When user enters "wrongusername" in username field
   And user enters "123456" in password field
   And user clicks Sign in button
   Then user gets login failed error message

Scenario: login fail - wrong password
   Given user is on Application landing page
   When user clicks on Sign in button
   Then user is displayed login screen
   When user enters "ShankarGarg" in username field
   And user enters "wrongpassword" in password field
   And user clicks Sign in button
   Then user gets login failed error message
```

In terms of syntax, there is no problem in this code. Cucumber will treat it as well as any other, but the problem is for the person writing the Feature file. If you look closely, only the dataset is changing and all the other Steps are the same. These are the following problems with this approach to creating Feature files:

- ► Copying and pasting Scenarios to use different values can quickly become tedious and repetitive.

- ► If tomorrow only one Step changes, it has to be changed in all the Scenarios. So, maintainability and reusability are big issues.

To avoid these problems, let's look at the next section and understand how we can solve them.

## How to do it...

Here, we are going to use the `Scenario Outline` keyword and add one Scenario Outline to test possible login Scenarios:

```
Scenario Outline: Login fail - possible combinations
    Given user is on Application landing page
    When user clicks on Sign in button
    Then user is displayed login screen
    When user enters "<UserName>" in username field
    And user enters "<Password>" in password field
    And user clicks Sign in button
    Then user gets login failed error message

    Examples:
      | UserName      | Password      |
      | wrongusername | 123456        |
      | ShankarGarg   | wrongpassword |
      | wrongusername | wrongpassword |
```

## How it works...

Here we have used the `Scenario Outline` keyword and we have merged all three Scenarios in to one Scenario Outline. One advantage of the Scenario Outline is that our Feature file is now compact and expressive. Let's understand Scenario Outline in more detail:

- ► Scenario Outline allow us to send test data to Scenarios through the use of a template with placeholders.

- ► A Scenario Outline is run once for each row in the Examples section beneath it (not counting the first row of column headers).

- ► A Scenario Outline is a template that is never directly run. It uses placeholders, which are contained within < > in the Scenario Outline's Steps.

▸ Think of a placeholder like a variable. It is replaced with a real value from the `Examples` table row, where the text between the placeholder's angle brackets matches that of the table column header.

  ❑ In the first execution, when Cucumber encounters the first Step with placeholders, which is `When user enters <UserName> in username field` in our case, Cucumber looks for a column with the header `UserName` in the `Examples` table.

  ❑ If there is no column with `UserName` in the `Examples` table, then Cucumber does not give an error but instead considers `<UserName>` as a String and passes it to Step Definition as it is.

  ❑ If Cucumber finds a column with the header `UserName`, then it picks the first row data from this column and replaces `UserName` with that value, which is `wrongusername` in our case, and sends this value to Step Definition.

  ❑ Cucumber repeats this process for all `< >` for one round of execution.

  ❑ So, for the first execution, this is how our Scenario Outline will look:

```
Given user is on Application landing page
When user clicks on Sign in button
Then user is displayed login screen
When user enters "wrongusername" in username field
And user enters "123456" in password field
And user clicks Sign in button
Then user gets login failed error message
```

▸ The value substituted for the placeholder changes with each subsequent run of the Scenario Outline. The values from the second row are taken for the second execution and so on, until the end of the `Examples` table is reached.

▸ The Scenario Outline itself is useless without an `Examples` table, which Lists the rows of values to be substituted for each placeholder.

Now that you have leaned the concept of Scenario Outline, try implementing the following:

▸ Write a Scenario Outline with multiple arguments in one Step.

▸ Can you create a Scenario Outline with multiple examples? You can group examples of positive tests and negative tests in different tables.

# Creating a Feature file in a language other than English

Most of us have worked in teams spanning multiple geographies, and we would agree that some of us are more comfortable in native languages as compared to English. We are able to express ourselves better, and we are also able to express everything. So what if our BA or PO is more comfortable in Danish compared to English? Let's write the specification in a language other than English in Cucumber.

## How to do it...

This is a sample English Feature file, which we will convert into different languages.

```
Feature: sample application
    In order to test login page
    As a Registered user
    I want to specify the login conditions

    Scenario: sample scenario
        Given user is on application page
        When user clicks login button
        Then user is on home page
```

To create the Feature file in Danish (`Danish.feature`):

```
# language: da
Egenskab: prøve ansøgning
      For at teste login side
      Som registreret bruger
      Jeg ønsker at angive login betingelser

    Scenarie: prøve scenario
        Givet brugeren er på ansøgning side
        Når brugeren klikker login knap
        Så Derefter bruger er på hjemmesiden
```

## How it works...

Cucumber allows us to write Feature files in around 40 spoken languages, thus empowering the teams whose first language is not English to write Feature files which are as robust as English language Feature files. The header `# language: da` in the first line of the Feature tells Cucumber what language will be used in the Feature file. By default, the language is English. If we want to write Feature files in another language, the Feature files must be saved with `"UTF-8"` encoding.

In a single project, we can have Feature files in multiple languages; but for one Feature file, only one language will work.

 For all languages, there is no difference in how Step definitions are generated.

# Combining Scenarios, Backgrounds, and Scenario Outlines

Until now we have learned about Scenarios, Steps, Background, and Scenario Outline individually. But when a BA or a PO has to write the Feature file, they have to combine all these keywords to come up with a very efficient and expressive Feature file.

Consider writing a Feature file for a login functionality where the latter meets the following criteria:

- ▸ The user should get an option to log in from the application's home page
- ▸ To log in, a user should have a username and password
- ▸ After a successful login, the user should be redirected to the home page
- ▸ In case of an unsuccessful login, the user should get the appropriate message
- ▸ The user should also get an option to register new users on the home page
- ▸ The user should also be able to verify which users exist in the application (this Feature is not present on the GitHub landing page but has been added for to clarify concepts)

 All these requirements are specific to the behavior of the application, and none of them are concerned with how you implement these requirements.

## How to do it...

Now we are going to use all the keywords we have explored until now, and we are going to create a `login.feature` file that specifies all the aforementioned requirements:

```
Feature: login Page
  In order to test login page
  As a Registered user
  I want to specify the login conditions

  Scenario: login flow
    Given user is on Application landing page
    And Sign in button is present on screen
    When user clicks on Sign in button
    Then user is displayed login screen
    When user enters "ShankarGarg" in username field
    And user enters "123456" in password field
    And user clicks Sign in button
    Then user is on home page
    And title of home page is "GitHub"

  Scenario Outline: Login fail - possible combinations
    Given user is on Application landing page
    When user clicks on Sign in button
    Then user is displayed login screen
    When user enters "<UserName>" in username field
    And user enters "<Password>" in password field
    And user clicks Sign in button
    Then user gets login failed error message

    Examples:
      | UserName      | Password      |
      | wrongusername | 123456        |
      | ShankarGarg   | wrongpassword |
      | wrongusername | wrongpassword |

  Scenario: Existing user Verification
    Given user is on Application landing page
    Then we verify following user exists
      | Name    | Email           | Phone |
      | Shankar | sgarg@email.com | 999   |
      | Ram     | ram@email.com   | 888   |
      | Sham    | sham@email.org  | 666   |
```

```
Scenario: New User Registration
  Given user is on Application landing page
  When user enters "ShankarGarg" in username field
  And user enters "sgarg@gmail.com" in password field
  And user enters "123456" in password field
  And user clicks on Signup for GitHub button
  Then user is successfully registered
```

## How it works...

Here we have combined all the keywords and concepts discussed until now in this chapter. Let's go through each requirement one by one and analyze how and with which keyword we specified these requirements:

- ▶ User should get an option to log in from the application home page—Scenario

- ▶ For login, a user should have a username and password—Scenario

- ▶ After successful login, the user should be redirected to the home page—Scenario

- ▶ In case of unsuccessful login, the user should get the appropriate message—Scenario Outline

- ▶ The user should also get an option to register new users on the home page—Scenario

- ▶ The user should also be able to verify which users exist in the application—Data Table

# 2

# Creating Step Definitions

In this chapter, we will cover the following topics:

- ▶ Creating your first Step Definitions file
- ▶ Identifying duplicate and Ambiguous Step Definitions
- ▶ Using regular expressions to optimize Step Definitions
- ▶ Using Optional Capture/Noncapture groups
- ▶ Transforming Data Tables to parse the test data
- ▶ Implementing Data Table diffs to compare tables
- ▶ Using Doc Strings to parse big data as one chunk
- ▶ Combining Doc Strings and Scenario Outlines
- ▶ Defining String transformations for better conversions

## Introduction

Sometimes people who are not that well versed in Cucumber argue that creating a Step Definitions file is an overhead as compared to the frameworks that do not have Cucumber. But what they don't realize is that Cucumber auto-generates these Step Definitions, so it's not an overhead. With the knowledge of the concepts covered in this chapter, you will be able to write very effective and efficient Step Definitions.

In this chapter, we will start with the basic concepts of Glue Code/Step Definitions in detail by covering the different types of Step Definitions, the usage of regular expressions, and so on. To come up with optimized and efficient Step Definitions, we will also elaborate upon advanced concepts of Doc Strings, Data Table transformations, and Capture groups.

# Creating your first Step Definitions file

Now let's assume you are an automation developer and you have to implement automated test cases for a Feature file. The next Step in this direction would be to write the Step Definitions for this Feature file. So, how do we write Step Definitions in a Cucumber project? Let's see how to do this in this recipe.

## How to do it...

The easiest way to create Step Definitions is to let Cucumber take care of it. The Steps are as follows:

1.  Here is the Feature file used in our previous chapter. Let's use this Feature file to create our first Step Definitions:

```
Feature: login Page
   In order to test login page
   As a Registered user
   I want to specify the login conditions

   Scenario: checking pre-condition, action and results
      Given user is on Application landing page
      When user clicks Sign in button
      Then user is on login screen
```

2. When you save the Feature file and run (either via Eclipse or via a Terminal), Cucumber is going to give errors for the missing Step Definition files along with suggestions for Step Definitions. An example of the errors shown in Eclipse is seen in the following screenshot:

```
WARNING: Cucumber-JVM's --format option is deprecated. Please use --plugin instead.
Feature: login Page
  In order to test login page
  As a Registered user
  I want to specify the login conditions

  Scenario: checking pre-condition, action and results # C:/Users/user/Documents/Xebia/Do
    Given user is on Application landing page
    When user clicks Sign in button
    Then user is on login screen

1 Scenarios (1 undefined)
3 Steps (3 undefined)
0m0.000s


You can implement missing steps with the snippets below:

@Given("^user is on Application landing page$")
public void user_is_on_Application_landing_page() throws Throwable {
    // Write code here that turns the phrase above into concrete actions
    throw new PendingException();
}

@When("^user clicks Sign in button$")
public void user_clicks_Sign_in_button() throws Throwable {
    // Write code here that turns the phrase above into concrete actions
    throw new PendingException();
}

@Then("^user is on login screen$")
public void user_is_on_login_screen() throws Throwable {
    // Write code here that turns the phrase above into concrete actions
    throw new PendingException();
}
```

3. Notice the suggestion given by Cucumber (highlighted in the preceding screenshot). As per Cucumber, all the Steps are in an **undefined** state as of now.

4. Copy the suggestions given by Cucumber and paste them to a default Step Definition file.

 Remember to give the path of the Step Definitions files to the Cucumber Options class.

5.  This is how our `LoginSteps.java` class will look:

```java
package com.StepDefinitions;

import cucumber.api.PendingException;
import cucumber.api.java.en.Given;
import cucumber.api.java.en.Then;
import cucumber.api.java.en.When;

public class LoginSteps {

  @Given("^user is on Application landing page$")
  public void user_is_on_Application_landing_page() throws
    Throwable {
      /* Write code here that turns the phrase above into
         concrete actions*/
    throw new PendingException();
  }

  @When("^user clicks Sign in button$")
  public void user_clicks_Sign_in_button() throws
    Throwable {
      /*Write code here that turns the phrase above into
         concrete actions */
    throw new PendingException();
  }

  @Then("^user is on login screen$")
  public void user_is_on_login_screen() throws Throwable {
      /* Write code here that turns the phrase above into
         concrete actions */
    throw new PendingException();
  }
}
```

6. Now, run the Feature file again and look at the Cucumber output:

```
WARNING: Cucumber-JVM's --format option is deprecated. Please use --plugin instead.
Feature: login Page
  In order to test login page
  As a Registered user
  I want to specify the login conditions

  Scenario: checking pre-condition, action and results # C:/Users/user/Documents/Xebia/Docs/cucumber/E
    Given user is on Application landing page         # LoginSteps.user_is_on_Application_landing_pag
      cucumber.api.PendingException: TODO: implement me
        at com.StepDefinitions.LoginSteps.user_is_on_Application_landing_page(LoginSteps.java:13)
        at ⊠.Given user is on Application landing page(C:/Users/user/Documents/Xebia/Docs/cucumber/Bod

    When user clicks Sign in button                   # LoginSteps.user_clicks_Sign_in_button()
    Then user is on login screen                      # LoginSteps.user_is_on_login_screen()

1 Scenarios (1 pending)
3 Steps (2 skipped, 1 pending)
0m0.129s

cucumber.api.PendingException: TODO: implement me
        at com.StepDefinitions.LoginSteps.user_is_on_Application_landing_page(LoginSteps.java:13)
        at ⊠.Given user is on Application landing page(C:/Users/user/Documents/Xebia/Docs/cucumber/Bod
```

7. Now our Scenario state has changed from **undefined** to **pending**. Refer to the highlighted area in the preceding screenshot. Cucumber suggests that we add the implementation to the pending Steps.

8. We will delete the throw statements from our class and replace them with some dummy code. You can call the actual automation code (either Selenium functions for websites or HTTPClient functions for service-oriented architecture (SOA) automation). Here is what our `LoginSteps.java` class looks like:

```
package com.StepDefinitions;

import cucumber.api.java.en.Given;
import cucumber.api.java.en.Then;
import cucumber.api.java.en.When;

public class LoginSteps {

  @Given("^user is on Application landing page$")
  public void user_is_on_Application_landing_page() throws
    Throwable {
    //sample code goes here
    System.out.println("Given");
  }

  @When("^user clicks Sign in button$")
  public void user_clicks_Sign_in_button() throws
    Throwable {
```

```
    //sample Code goes here
    System.out.println("When");
}

@Then("^user is on login screen$")
public void user_is_on_login_screen() throws Throwable {
    //sample Code goes here
    System.out.println("Then");
}
}
```

9.  Now, execute the Feature file again and observe the Cucumber output:

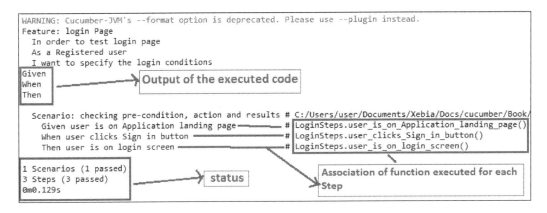

10. Now the Cucumber output has changed and the status of our Steps has changed from **pending** to **passed**; also, the output of each function called in each Step has also been printed.

> Whether a Step Definitions was created with the annotations @Given, @When, or @Then, a Step Definitions will match any Gherkin Step as long as the regular expression matches the main text of the Step. For example, Given I have 100 in my account and When I have 100 in my account will be matched to @Given("^I have (.*?) in my account$").

## How it works...

Now let's understand each Step performed in the previous section in more detail to get a better understanding of the concept of Step Definitions:

# Step Definitions

- ▸ When Cucumber starts execution, it looks for all classes on the Classpath that are in a specified glue package (or descendant).

- ▸ A Step Definitions is a small piece of code with a pattern attached to it. The pattern is used to link the Step Definitions to all the matching Steps, and the code is what Cucumber will execute when it sees a Gherkin Step.

- ▸ We use Cucumber annotations, such as @Given, @When, and @Then to create Step Definitions.

- ▸ In the Step Given user is on Application landing page, the text after the Given keyword (user is on Application landing page) is what Cucumber matches in the Step Definitions file (**@Given("^user is on Application landing page$")**). And when Cucumber finds a match, it executes the function mentioned within that Step.

# Undefined Steps

- ▸ When we first executed the Feature file, Cucumber did not find any matching Step Definitions, that's why Cucumber gave us **Undefined Steps Error**.

- ▸ Cucumber will also give its own Suggestion for getting rid of Undefined Steps. All subsequent Steps after Undefined Step in the Scenario are skipped and Scenario is marked as Fail.

# Pending Steps

- ▸ When we use the code suggested by Cucumber in our Step Definition file, and we run the Feature file then we get Pending Steps Exception.

- ▸ Pending Steps Exception is because of following Code:

```
throw new PendingException();
```

- ▸ When Cucumber encounters this statement, it understands that these Steps are still a work in progress Step.

- ▸ Status of the Scenario is pending, First Step having PendingException() will be marked as pending and all other Steps in that Scenario are skipped.

# Implemented Steps

- ▸ When we replace the throw command with functional code, the pending exception error goes away.

- ▸ Now, the status of the Steps will depend on the code being executed in that Step.

# Identifying Duplicate and Ambiguous Step Definitions

Sometimes when we are writing Cucumber Step Definitions files, we get either Duplicate Step Definitions errors or Ambiguous Step Definitions errors. Let's try and understand the reasons why these errors arise, and how we can remove them through this recipe.

## How to do it...

We will use the same Feature file from previous recipe. Perform the following Steps:

1. Let's create one more class in the `StepDefinitions` package, called `DuplicateAmbiguous.java`, with the following content:

```java
package com.StepDefinitions;

import cucumber.api.java.en.Given;

public class DuplicateAmbiguous {

  //Duplicate Steps
  @Given("^user is on Application landing page$")
  public void
    user_is_on_Application_landing_page_duplicate()
      throws Throwable {
    //sample code goes here
    System.out.println("Duplicate");
  }

}
```

When you try to run the Feature file, observe the Cucumber output:

```
Exception in thread "main"
cucumber.runtime.DuplicateStepDefinitionException: Duplicate
Step Definitions in
com.StepDefinitions.DuplicateAmbiguous.user_is_on_Application_
landing_page_duplicate() in
file:/C:/Users/user/Documents/Xebia/Docs/cucumber/Book/Project
/target/test-classes/ and
com.StepDefinitions.LoginSteps.user_is_on_Application_landing_
page() in
file:/C:/Users/user/Documents/Xebia/Docs/cucumber/Book/Project
/target/test-classes/

    at
cucumber.runtime.RuntimeGlue.addStepDefinition(RuntimeGlue.jav
```

```
a:33)
    at
cucumber.runtime.java.JavaBackend.addStepDefinition(JavaBacken
d.java:153)
    at
cucumber.runtime.java.MethodScanner.scan(MethodScanner.java:68
)
    at
cucumber.runtime.java.MethodScanner.scan(MethodScanner.java:41
)
    at
cucumber.runtime.java.JavaBackend.loadGlue(JavaBackend.java:89
)
    at cucumber.runtime.Runtime.<init>(Runtime.java:90)
    at cucumber.runtime.Runtime.<init>(Runtime.java:68)
    at cucumber.runtime.Runtime.<init>(Runtime.java:64)
    at cucumber.api.cli.Main.run(Main.java:35)
    at cucumber.api.cli.Main.main(Main.java:18)
```

2. Cucumber gives us a Duplicate Step Definitions error stating that there are two Step Definitions that are an exact match.

3. Let's change the content of DuplicateAmbiguous.java to the following code:

```java
package com.StepDefinitions;

import cucumber.api.java.en.Given;

public class DuplicateAmbiguous {

   //Ambiguous Steps
   @Given("^user is on (.*?) page$")
   public void
     user_is_on_Application_landing_page_ambiguous()
       throws Throwable {
       //sample code goes here
     System.out.println("Duplicate");
   }

}
```

4. Now run the Feature file and observe the Cucumber output:

```
   Scenario: checking pre-condition, action and results #
C:/Users/user/Documents/Xebia/Docs/cucumber/Book/Project/
src/test/java/com/features/login.feature:6
   Given user is on Application landing page          #
DuplicateAmbiguous.user_is_on_Application_landing_page_
ambiguous()
      cucumber.runtime.AmbiguousStepDefinitionsException:
⬚.Given user is on Application landing
page(C:/Users/user/Documents/Xebia/Docs/cucumber/Book/
Project/src/test/java/com/features/login.feature:7) matches
more than one Step Definition:
      ^user is on (.*?) page$ in
DuplicateAmbiguous.user_is_on_Application_landing_page_
ambiguous()
      ^user is on Application landing page$ in
LoginSteps.user_is_on_Application_landing_page()

      at
cucumber.runtime.RuntimeGlue.stepDefinitionMatch
(RuntimeGlue.java:71)
      at cucumber.runtime.Runtime.runStep
(Runtime.java:265)
      at cucumber.runtime.model.StepContainer.runStep
(StepContainer.java:44)
      at cucumber.runtime.model.StepContainer.runSteps
(StepContainer.java:39)
      at cucumber.runtime.model.CucumberScenario.run
(CucumberScenario.java:48)
      at cucumber.runtime.model.CucumberFeature.run
(CucumberFeature.java:163)
      at cucumber.runtime.Runtime.run(Runtime.java:120)
      at cucumber.api.cli.Main.run(Main.java:36)
      at cucumber.api.cli.Main.main(Main.java:18)
```

```
    When user clicks Sign in button                    #
LoginSteps.user_clicks_Sign_in_button()
    Then user is on login screen                       #
LoginSteps.user_is_on_login_screen()


1 Scenarios (1 failed)
3 Steps (1 failed, 2 skipped)
0m0.000s
```

5.  Here, Cucumber throws the Ambiguous Steps error and is not able to decide which Step Definitions to use, as the two Step Definitions are a partial match.

## How it works...

Since Cucumber-JVM looks for all classes on the Classpath that are in a specified glue package (or descendant), so there are chances that we might have some duplication (partial/exact) in Step Definitions. Let's understand this in more detail:

 ▸ **Duplicate Steps**: When Cucumber encounters multiple Step Definitions that are exactly the same, it throws a Duplicate Step Definitions exception.

 ▸ **Ambiguous Steps**: When Cucumber encounters multiple Step Definitions that are a partial match, it throws an Ambiguous Step Definitions exception.

If Cucumber encounters duplicate/Ambiguous Steps, all the other Steps of such Scenarios are skipped and those Scenarios are marked as Fail.

Cucumber even specifies the two instances that are causing the error (refer to the highlighted code in the Cucumber output shown in Step 4 of this recipe).

In one execution, only the first two occurrences of the erroneous Steps are identified; if there are more duplicate occurrences of the same Step, then these will be identified in the next execution.

To check that there are no errors or exceptions in the Step Definitions, run Feature files with `dryRun = true` and `strict=true` in the Cucumber Options class. This will only check the validity of the Step Definitions and will not execute the code within them. We will read about these options in detail in later chapters.

# Using Regular Expressions to optimize Step Definitions

Until now, we have created Step Definitions with one-to-one relations with Steps. But this way of writing Step Definitions can be cumbersome as we write more and more Feature files. So, we will write generic Step Definitions that will apply to all the Steps that follow a certain pattern, thus bringing down the number of Step Definitions required. Let's see how to do this in this recipe.

## How to do it...

1.  Let's assume we are writing Step Definitions for the following Scenario.

    ```
    Scenario: login fail - wrong username
        Given user is displayed login screen
        When user enters "wrongusername" in username field
        And user enters "123456" in password field
        And user clicks Sign in button
    ```

2.  Now run the Feature file, and copy and paste the Cucumber Step Definitions suggestions in the `LoginSteps.java` class. This is how `LoginSteps.java` looks:

    ```java
    package com.StepDefinitions;

    import cucumber.api.java.en.Given;
    import cucumber.api.java.en.When;

    public class LoginSteps {

      @Given("^user is displayed login screen$")
      public void user_is_displayed_login_screen()  {
      }

      @When("^user enters \"(.*?)\" in username field$")
      public void user_enters_in_username_field(String
        username) {
        System.out.println(username);
      }

      @When("^user enters \"(.*?)\" in password field$")
      public void user_enters_in_password_field(String
        password)  {
        System.out.println(password);
      }
    ```

```
@When("^user clicks Sign in button$")
public void user_clicks_Sign_in_button() {
}
}
```

3. Focus on the Step Definitions mentioned in bold in the preceding code sample. We have used regular expressions and enabled a single Step Definitions to match various Steps, which matches the wildcard pattern mentioned.

## How it works...

Cucumber allows us to use regular expressions to empower Step Definitions to match multiple Steps. Let's understand how this works:

▸ **Capture groups:**

When you surround part of a regular expression with parentheses, it becomes a capture group. In a Cucumber Step Definitions, the text matched within each capture group is passed to the code block as an argument.

For example in 2nd Step Definition Capture group is `wrongusername` and it will be passed to variable username. Similarly in 3rd Step Definition Capture Group is `password` and it will be passed to variable password.

For statically typed languages, Cucumber will automatically transforms those Strings into the appropriate type. For dynamically typed languages, no transformation happens by default, as there is no type information.

▸ Cucumber also allows integers to be passed in Capture groups.

For example, consider the following Step:

```
Given I have 58 Dollars in my account
```

For this Step, the Step Definitions will look like this (focus on the highlighted code):

```
@Given("I have (\\d+) Dollars in my account")
  public void I_have_dollar_acnt(int dollar) {
    // Do something with the dollars
  }
```

▸ Cucumber also allows Lists to be passed in Capture groups.

For example, consider the following Step:

```
Given I am available on "Tuesday,Friday,Sunday"
```

Step Definition will look like this, focus on the highlighted code:

```
@Given("^I am available on \"(.+)\"$")
public void i_am_available_on(List<String> days)  {
System.out.println(days.size());
}
```

The following are some types of regular expressions available in Cucumber:

- **. Dot** means match any single character.
- **\* Star**, a repetition modifier, takes a character and tells us how many times it can reappear.
- **+ Plus**, a repetition modifier, takes a character and tells us that the character can be repeated at least once.
- **\d** stands for diGitHub, or [0-9].
- **\w** stands for a word character, specifically [A-Za-z0-9_].
- **\s** stands for a whitespace character, including tab space or line break.

> You can also negate shorthand character classes by capitalizing them; for example, \D refers to any character except a diGitHub.

# Using Optional Capture and Noncapture Groups

Until now, we have covered how to write Step Definitions for various keywords in Feature files. Now let's talk about how we can efficiently use Step Definitions for multiple Steps.

Think about a situation where we are testing a positive situation in one Step and a negative situation in some other Step—the only difference in both Steps is just the word "No", while the remaining sentence is same. Based on the knowledge that we have acquired so far, we will write two Step Definitions for these two Steps. But is there a better way of doing this? Let's see how we can do this better in this recipe.

## How to do it...

1. For this recipe, consider the following Scenarios and focus on the highlighted text:

   ```
   Scenario: Optional Capture Groups/Alternation
        #positive
        Then I see following dollars in my account
        #negative
        Then I do not see following dollars in my account

        Scenario: Optional Non capture Groups
        Given I have following dollars in my account
        Given He has following dollars in my account
        Given User has following dollars in my account
   ```

   Use the following Step Definitions for both Scenarios and focus on the code that is highlighted:

   ```
   @Then("^I( do not see| see) following dollars in my
   account$")
   public void I_see_or_do_not_see_following_dollars_in_my_
   account(String seeOrDoNotSee) {
        //print the value of capture group
   System.out.println(seeOrDoNotSee);
   }

   @Given("^(?:I have|He has|User has) following dollars
        in my account$")
   public void have_following_dollars_in_my_account() {

        // Non Capture groups are not captured in Step
   }
   ```

2. Now run the Scenarios; you will see the following output:

```
Feature: Sample
Name
Email
Shankar                              Elements of the table passed in
sgarg@email.com                      Data Table
Ram
ram@email.com
Sham
sham@email.org

  Scenario: Existing user Verification    # C:/Users/user/Documents/Xebia/Docs/cucumber/Book/Project/
     Given user is displayed login screen # LoginSteps.user_is_displayed_login_screen()
     Then we verify following user exists # LoginSteps.we_verify_following_user_exists(DataTable)

1 Scenarios (1 passed)
2 Steps (2 passed)
0m0.130s
```

## How it works...

An Optional Capture group eliminates the duplication of Step Definitions and can definitely improve the readability of Feature files. Using optional groups, the same Step Definitions can be used for both positive and negative assertions. Let's discuss this in more detail:

 ▶  Optional Capture group/alternation:

   The use of a pipe between parentheses creates an optional group (Text1|Text 2). Here, more than two options can also be grouped. In this example, Steps with either Text1 or Text2 will be accepted by this Step Definitions, and accordingly, Text1 or Text2 will be passed as the Capture value.

 ▶  Optional Noncapture group:

   The addition of ?: to the beginning of Optional Capture groups creates optional non-Capture groups. Having ?: will treat the group as optional , but it will not be captured. So, you do not need to pass an argument as described earlier with optional captured groups.

# Transforming Data Tables to parse the test data

In the previous chapter, we covered how Data Tables can be used to send large sets of data to a single Step. Now let's understand how to handle Data Tables in Step Definitions in this recipe.

## How to do it...

1.  Let's assume we are writing Step Definitions for the following Scenario:

```
Scenario: Existing user Verification
    Given user is displayed login screen
    Then we verify following user exists
        | Name    | Email           |
        | Shankar | sgarg@email.com |
        | Ram     | ram@email.com   |
        | Sham    | sham@email.org  |
```

2.  Now run the Feature file, and copy paste the Cucumber Step Definitions suggestions in the LoginSteps.java class. These are the additional Steps in LoginSteps.java:

```
@Then("^we verify following user exists$")
public void we_verify_following_user_exists(DataTable arg1)
    throws Throwable {
```

```
    /* Write code here that turns the phrase above into
    concrete actions
    For automatic transformation, change DataTable to
    one of List<YourType>, List<List<E>>,
    List<Map<K,V>> or Map<K,V>.
    E,K,V must be a scalar (String, Integer, Date,
    enum etc) */
    throw new PendingException();
}
```

3. Here, Cucumber passed the table as `DataTable` to the Step argument. Focus on the suggestion given by Cucumber to convert the table to a List or a List of Lists and so on.

4. Now, replace the code suggestion given by Cucumber with the following code:

```
@Then("^we verify following user exists$")
public void we_verify_following_user_exists(DataTable
  userDetails) {

  List<List<String>> details = userDetails.raw();

  for (int i = 0; i < details.size(); i++) {
    for (int j = 0; j < details.get(i).size(); j++) {
    System.out.println(details.get(i).get(j));
    }
  }
}
```

Here, we have used the `raw()` method of the Cucumber DataTable API to convert the Data Table into a List of List of Strings. After that, we have used two `for` loops to traverse all the elements of the List of List of Strings. This is how the Cucumber output looks:

```
Feature: Sample
Name
Email                           Elements of the table passed in
Shankar                         Data Table
sgarg@email.com
Ram
ram@email.com
Sham
sham@email.org

  Scenario: Existing user Verification    # C:/Users/user/Documents/Xebia/Docs/cucumber/Book/Project/
    Given user is displayed login screen # LoginSteps.user_is_displayed_login_screen()
    Then we verify following user exists # LoginSteps.we_verify_following_user_exists(DataTable)

1 Scenarios (1 passed)
2 Steps (2 passed)
0m0.130s
```

## How it works...

Data Tables are passed to the Step Definitions as the last argument. We need to import `cucumber.api.DataTable` into Java code. DataTable API's `raw()` method is used to convert a Data Table to a List of List of String.

We can also convert a Data Table to various types of Lists. Let's see what we can do:

- **A List of user-defined variables**:

  Let's define a custom class called `User`, which has name and email as data members. The header row is used to name fields in a generic List type:

  ```
  public class User {
      public String name;
      public String email;
  }
  ```

  Now, its Step Definitions can be like this:

  ```
  @Then("^we verify following user exists$")
  public void we_verify_following_user_exists(List<User>
    userList) {
      for (User u : userList) {
        System.out.println(u.name);
      }
  }
  ```

  This Step Definitions will accept a List with objects as users (which is custom defined by us) and will print the names of users.

- **A List of maps**:

  Using the `User` class defined in the previous Step, the Step Definitions can be like this:

  ```
  @Then("^we verify following user exists$")
  public void
    we_verify_following_user_exists(List<Map<String, String>>
      userList) {
      for (Map<String, String> u : userList) {
        System.out.println(u.get("Name"));
      }
  }
  ```

  The Data Table is converted to the following List of maps:

  ```
  {Name=Shankar, Email=sgarg@email.com}
  {Name=Ram, Email=ram@email.com}
  {Name=Sham, Email=sham@email.org}
  ```

If you're converting a Data Table into a map, it is usually advisable not to have a top row naming the columns in the Gherkin table.

▸ **List of List of scalar:**

Using the `User` class defined in the previous Step, the Step Definitions can be presented as follows:

```
@Then("^we verify following user exists$")
public void
  we_verify_following_user_exists(List<List<String>>
    userList) {
    for (List<String> u : userList) {
      System.out.println(u);
    }
  }
```

The Data Table is converted to the following Lists:

```
[Name, Email]
[Shankar, sgarg@email.com]
[Ram, ram@email.com]
[Sham, sham@email.org]
```

# Implementing data table diffs to compare tables

Consider a situation where you need to verify an application response that is in the form of Table to another Data Table that we are sending in Feature file. This kind of verification is very common when we are testing REST services.

Based on what we have learned so far, we will break the Data Table down in the Feature file into a List of Lists, and then we will verify each element of those Lists with expected Lists (which we got after breaking the table). Let's understand how we can do this in an easier way.

## How to do it...

1.  For this recipe, consider the following Scenario:

```
Scenario: Table Diff
    Given user send a get request to "localhost:8080/e"
    Then user gets following response
```

```
| username | age |
| sham     | 25  |
| ram      | 26  |
```

2. Now save the Feature file. After adding the following code to suggestions, this is how our Step Definitions will look:

```
@Given("^user send a get request to \"(.*?)\"$")
public void user_send_a_get_request_to(String arg1) {
    // lets assume user sends a get request
}


@Then("^user gets following response$")
public void user_gets_following_response(DataTable
  expectedUsers) {

    /* lets create a table for system response
    (actualUsers) */
    List<List<String>> actualUsers = new
       ArrayList<List<String>>();
    actualUsers.add( Arrays.asList("username", "age"));
    actualUsers.add( Arrays.asList("sham", "25"));
    actualUsers.add( Arrays.asList("ram", "26"));

    /* Use the diff method to differentiate two data
    tables */
    expectedUsers.diff(actualUsers);
}
```

## How it works...

We can compare a table argument (the actual result) to another table that we provide within the Step Definitions (the expected result).

Both the tables should be in a certain format for it to work properly. Both tables should be column-oriented, and the first row of both tables should represent the column names. The column names must be unique for each column and they must match.

If the tables are different, an exception is thrown, and the difference between the two tables is reported in the execution report. Its output will look like this:

```
Scenario: Table Diff                              # C:/Users/user/Documents/Xebia/Docs/cucumber/Book/Pr
  Given user send a get request to "localhost:8080/e"  # LoginSteps.user_send_a_get_request_to(String)
  Then user gets following response               # LoginSteps.user_gets_following_response(DataTable)
  ┌─────────────────────────────────────────────────────────────┐
  │ cucumber.runtime.table.TableDiffException: Tables were not identical:         Difference shown by +
  │    - │ username │ age      │                                                  and -
  │    + │ username │ password │
  │      │ sham     │ 25       │
  │      │ ram      │ 26       │
  └─────────────────────────────────────────────────────────────┘
      at cucumber.runtime.table.TableDiffer.calculateDiffs(TableDiffer.java:38)
      at cucumber.api.DataTable.diff(DataTable.java:178)
      at cucumber.api.DataTable.diff(DataTable.java:168)
      at com.StepDefinitions.LoginSteps.user_gets_following_response(LoginSteps.java:116)
      at ▢.Then user gets following response(C:/Users/user/Documents/Xebia/Docs/cucumber/Book/Project/src/t
```

Rows that differ from what was expected will be printed twice—the first (preceded by a "-") is what was expected, followed by another (preceded by a "+"), which is what was actually returned.

# Using Doc Strings to parse big data as one chunk

Now let's consider a situation where we have to specify a lot of text in multiple lines (not in the shape of a table)—something like a few lines from a blog or a book. So, how do we handle this in Step Definitions? This is called passing Doc Strings in test Steps. Based on what we have covered until now, we can use regular expressions; but this is helpful for the first line only, and the text in all the other lines will be missed. In this recipe, let's see how to handle this situation.

## How to do it...

1. Let's consider the following Step in our Feature file for this exercise:

```
Given a book named "cucumber cookbook" with following body
    """
    Title - Cucumber cookbook
    Author of this book is first time writer so please excuse
        the naïve mistakes. But he will definitely improve
            with chapters he writes.
    """
```

   Here, the highlighted text is the Doc String that we will be passing to the Step Definitions.

2. Save and run the Feature file, and copy and paste the Cucumber suggestion for the missing Step Definitions. After adding the print statements, this is how our code will look:

```
@Given("^a book named \"(.*?)\" with following body$")
public void a_book_named_with_following_body(String arg1,
    String arg2) {
```

```
        //prints the regular expression
        System.out.println(arg1);

        //prints the Doc String
        System.out.println(arg2);
    }
```

3. This is the output of the preceding code:

```
Feature: Sample
cucumber cookbook          Regular Expression - String                        Doc String
Title - Cucumber cookbook
Author of this book is first time writer so please excuse the naïve mistakes. But he will definitely

    Scenario: Existing user Verification                          # C:/Users/user/Documents/Xebia/Docs/c
        Given a book named "cucumber cookbook" with following body # LoginSteps.a_book_named_with_followi
        """
        Title - Cucumber cookbook
        Author of this book is first time writer so please excuse the naïve mistakes. But he will defin
        """


1 Scenarios (1 passed)
1 Steps (1 passed)
0m0.127s
```

## How it works...

When writing Feature files, Doc Strings should be within three adjacent quotes " " " at the beginning and three at the end.

In Step Definitionss, you don't have to do anything special for Doc Strings, as the text within triple quotes (" " ") will be passed as the last argument to the Step Definitions. In our code, we have also used one regular expression for the text Cucumber Cookbook, but not for the Doc String as the Doc String was passed to the last argument of the Step.

Indentation of the opening """ is unimportant, although common practice is to put it two spaces in from the enclosing Step. Each line of the String passed in the Doc String will be realigned to the indentation of the opening """.

# Combining Doc Strings and Scenario Outlines

Now think of a situation where you are passing a Doc String but you have to combine that with a Scenario Outline. How does Cucumber behave in such a situation?

Let's think of a situation where we are specifying the requirements for the content of an e-mail, but the content is based on the role from which the e-mail is sent. So how do we specify such a requirement in a Feature file and how do we write the Step Definitions for it? Let's find out in this recipe.

## How to do it...

1. For this recipe, let's consider this Scenario:

```
Scenario Outline: E-mail content verification
    Given I have a user account with <Role> rights
    Then I should receive an email with the body:
    """
    Dear user,
    You have been granted <Role> rights.  You are
      <details>. Please be
    responsible.
    -The Admins
    """

    Examples:
      | Role    | details                                 |
      | Manager | now able to manage your employee accounts |
      | Admin   | able to manage any user account on system |
```

2. Now run the Feature file; copy the Step Definitions suggestion given by Cucumber and replace it with the following Step Definitions:

```
@Given("^I have a user account with (.*?) rights$")
public void
   i_have_a_user_account_with_Manager_rights(String role) {

   //prints the role
   System.out.println(role);

}


@Then("^I should receive an email with the body:$")
public void i_should_receive_an_email_with_the_body(String
   docString) {
```

```
/* prints the content of Doc String with Scenario
outlineSubstitution */
System.out.println(docString);
}
```

3.  When you run the Scenario, this is the output for the data substitution of Row 1:

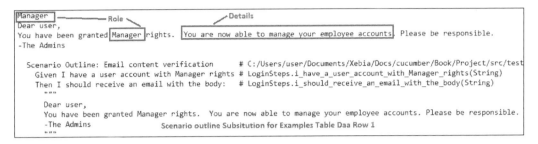

And this is the output for the data substitution of Row 2:

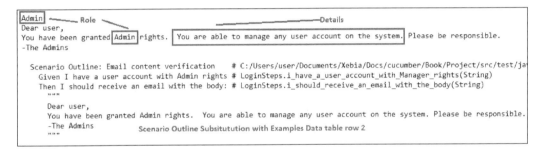

How it works...

In the preceding section, you learned how two basic concepts can be combined to come up with a solution for a complex problem. Two concepts that we used here are Doc Strings and Scenario Outline. Let's see how they work:

If you look closely, the highlighted text which is within <> in the Then Step of the Scenario Outline in Step 1 is the same as the text in the example table header row. (The text has been highlighted in Step 1). So, we are telling Cucumber that this text is just a placeholder, and during execution, its value will come from the example table.

As we have seen in the preceding recipe, we don't have to do anything special for Doc Strings in Step Definitions—they are automatically passed as the last argument. So we did not have to do anything special in Step 2.

Now in Step 3, you can see in the output of the first execution: the values of <Role> and <details> are replaced with the data from Data Row 1 of the example table, and in the second execution, the values are replaced with data from Data Row 2 of the example table.

# Defining String transformations for better conversions

Think about a Scenario where you want to convert some Strings in test Steps to some specific Strings in your code. For example, the PO has mentioned "29-12-1986" in a Step and you want Cucumber to understand this text as a date. Further, in some countries this could be in the DD-MM-YYYY format, while in others, it could be in the MM-DD-YYYY format. So how do we standardize this conversion? Let's find out how we can do this in Cucumber.

## Getting ready

Consider the following test Step for this problem:

```
Given My Birthday is on "29-12-1986"
```

Now, we can use the `@Format` String transformer to convert text to date.

## How to do it...

Import `java.util.Date` into your Step Definitions file. This is how our Step Definitions will look:

```
@Given("^My Birthday is on \"(.*?)\"$")
  public void my_Birthday_is_on(@Format("dd-MM-yyyy") Date
    bday) {
    //prints the text converted to Java.util.Date
    System.out.println(bday);

    //prints the class of bday to confirm it's a Date
    System.out.println(bday.getClass());
  }
```

This is the output that appears after running the preceding Step:

```
Feature: Sample
Mon Dec 29 00:00:00 IST 1986          29-12-1986 converted to
class java.util.Date                  java.util.date

   Scenario: Existing user Verification   # C:/Users/user/Documents/Xebia/Docs/cucumb
      Given My Birthday is on "29-12-1986" # LoginSteps.my_Birthday_is_on(Date)

1 Scenarios (1 passed)
1 Steps (1 passed)
0m0.125s
```

## How it works...

Cucumber-JVM allows converting Strings into various scalar types. A scalar type is a type that can be derived from a single String value. Some of Cucumber-JVM's built-in scalar types are `numbers, enums, java.util.Date, java.util.Calendar`, and so on. Transformation to `java.util.Date` and `java.util.Calendar` will work out-of-the-box as long as the String value matches one of the Short, Medium, Full, or Long formats defined by `java.util.DateFormat`.

`29-12-1986` from our example doesn't match any of those formats, so we have to give Cucumber a hint by using `@Format`. We need to specify two things: First is the Format and second is the Data Type.

We can also write custom formatters if the formatting is not available in Cucumber-JVM by default. Further, we can even use String transformation for in cases other than date transformations.

# 3
# Enabling Fixtures

In this chapter, we will cover the following topics:

- ▸ Tagging
- ▸ ANDing and ORing Tags
- ▸ Adding Hooks to Cucumber code
- ▸ Tagging the Hooks
- ▸ ANDing and ORing the Tagged Hooks

## Introduction

In this chapter, we will discuss how to get control of what Features to run, and when to run them; for example, we may want to run only one set of Feature files like Sanity, or we may want to take a screenshot after each Scenario. This type of control is called **fixtures**. Cucumber allows us to enable fixtures via the concepts of Tags and Hooks. With knowledge of the concepts covered in this chapter, you will be able to write very effective and efficient fixtures.

In this chapter, we will start with basic concepts of Tags and Hooks followed by ANDing and ORing them. Then we will cover the power of Tag and Hook combinations.

## Tagging

Let's assume you are an automation architect and you have to run a specific set of Scenarios or Feature files. This situation may occur often: let's say we have made changes to one functionality and now we want to run Features/Scenarios of that functionality only.

Now let's understand how we can Tag some Scenarios as Sanity, some as Regression, and some as both. Let's see in our next section.

Now, there is the `home_page.feature` file and we want to Tag it as important. We also want to Tag some Scenarios as `sanity` and some as `regression` or some as both. So, how do we do this in a Cucumber project? Let's see in our next section.

## Getting ready

Let's use the following Feature file for this recipe:

```
Feature: Home Page

    Background: flow till home page
        Given user is on Application home page

    Scenario: Home Page Default content
        Then user gets a GitHub Bootcamp section

    Scenario: GitHub Bootcamp Section
        When user focuses on GitHub Bootcamp Section
        Then user gets an option to setup git

    Scenario: Top Banner content
        When user focuses on Top Banner
        Then user gets an option of home page
```

## How to do it...

1.  We need to simply write `@sanity` or `@regression` before the Scenario and `@important` in front of the Feature file. Refer to the highlighted text in the code. This is how our updated `home_page.feature` file should look:

    **@important**
    ```
    Feature: Home Page

        Background: flow till home page
            Given user is on Application home page

    ```
    **@sanity**
    ```
        Scenario: Home Page Default content
            Then user gets a GitHub Bootcamp section

    ```
    **@regression**
    ```
        Scenario: GitHub Bootcamp Section
            When user focuses on GitHub Bootcamp Section
            Then user gets an option to setup git
    ```

```
@sanity @regression
Scenario: Top Banner content
    When user focuses on Top Banner
    Then user gets an option of home page
```

2. Open the Command Prompt and go to the `project` directory.

3. Use the following command to run the Feature file that has been tagged as `important`:

**mvn test -Dcucumber.options="--tags @important"**

We will explore this command in detail in the next chapter—use it as it is for time being.

We will get this output:

```
-------------------------------------------------------
 T E S T S
-------------------------------------------------------
Running com.CucumberOptions.RunCukeTest
@important
Feature: Home Page

  Background: flow till home page          # sample.feature:4
    Given user is on Application home page # LoginSteps.user_is_on_Application_home_page()

  @sanity
  Scenario: Home Page Default content        # sample.feature:8
    Then user gets a github bootcamp section # LoginSteps.user_gets_a_github_bootcamp_section()

  Background: flow till home page          # sample.feature:4
    Given user is on Application home page # LoginSteps.user_is_on_Application_home_page()

  @regression
  Scenario: GitHub Bootcamp Section              # sample.feature:12
    When user focuses on GitHub Bootcamp Section # LoginSteps.user_focuses_on_GitHub_Bootcamp_Section()
    Then user gets an option to setup git        # LoginSteps.user_gets_an_option_to_setup_git()

  Background: flow till home page          # sample.feature:4
    Given user is on Application home page # LoginSteps.user_is_on_Application_home_page()

  @sanity @regression
  Scenario: Top Banner content             # sample.feature:17
    When user focuses on Top Banner        # LoginSteps.user_focuses_on_Top_Banner()
    Then user gets an option of home page  # LoginSteps.user_gets_an_option_of_home_page()

3 Scenarios (3 passed)
8 Steps (8 passed)
0m0.204s

Tests run: 11, Failures: 0, Errors: 0, Skipped: 0, Time elapsed: 0.926 sec
```

Although there are many Feature files in our project, only the Feature file that is Tagged as important is run, and that's why all the Scenarios were also run.

4. Now, run the following command in the command prompt:

```
mvn test -Dcucumber.options="--tags @sanity"
```

This is the output:

```
-------------------------------------------------
 T E S T S
-------------------------------------------------
Running com.CucumberOptions.RunCukeTest
@important
Feature: Home Page

  Background: flow till home page          # sample.feature:4
    Given user is on Application home page # LoginSteps.user_is_on_Application_home_page()

  @sanity
  Scenario: Home Page Default content      # sample.feature:8
    Then user gets a github bootcamp section # LoginSteps.user_gets_a_github_bootcamp_section()

  Background: flow till home page          # sample.feature:4
    Given user is on Application home page # LoginSteps.user_is_on_Application_home_page()

  @sanity @regression
  Scenario: Top Banner content             # sample.feature:17
    When user focuses on Top Banner        # LoginSteps.user_focuses_on_Top_Banner()
    Then user gets an option of home page  # LoginSteps.user_gets_an_option_of_home_page()

2 Scenarios (2 passed)
5 Steps (5 passed)
0m0.236s

Tests run: 7, Failures: 0, Errors: 0, Skipped: 0, Time elapsed: 0.981 sec

Results :

Tests run: 7, Failures: 0, Errors: 0, Skipped: 0
```

Now, only two Scenarios are executed and both the Scenarios that are executed are Tagged as `@sanity`. So it is clear that whichever Scenarios are mentioned while running Cucumber, only those Scenarios are run.

## How it works...

Tags are used to organize Feature files and Scenarios. You Tag a Scenario by putting a word prefixed with the @ character on the line before the `Scenario` keyword.

 A Feature/Scenario can have multiple Tags; just separate them with spaces or put them on a different line.

Inheritance is when Tags are inherited. If a Feature file has a Tag, then Cucumber will assign that Tag to all Scenarios and all Scenario Outlines in that Feature file.

You can customize your run by using `--tags` when running Cucumber test cases from the Terminal. A few examples are as follows:

▸ `mvn test -Dcucumber.options="--tags @important"` will run all Scenarios (because we are running a Tag associated with Feature).

▸ `mvn test -Dcucumber.options="--tags @sanity"` will run Scenarios associated with `@sanity`.

> The ~ special character in front of any Tag tells Cucumber to ignore all the Scenarios associated with that Tag.

▸ `mvn test -Dcucumber.options="--tags ~@important"` will run test cases that do not have the `@important` Tag associated with them.

# ANDing and ORing Tags

Most of the time, changes are made to many functionalities simultaneously; so it becomes imperative for testers to test all those functionalities. Sometimes we have to run all the Scenarios marked as `@sanity` and `@regression` and sometimes we want to run all Scenarios for `feature1` or `feature2`. So how do we do this in Cucumber? Let's see that in this section.

## Getting ready

This is the `Feature` file we will use for this recipe:

```
@important
Feature: Home Page

   Background: flow till home page
      Given user is on Application home page

   @sanity
   Scenario: Home Page Default content
      Then user gets a GitHub Bootcamp section

   @regression
   Scenario: GitHub Bootcamp Section
      When user focuses on GitHub Bootcamp Section
      Then user gets an option to setup git
```

```
@sanity @regression
Scenario: Top Banner content
   When user focuses on Top Banner
   Then user gets an option of home page
```

## How to do it...

1.  If we want to run the Scenarios which are Tagged `sanity` and `regression` both, then run the following command in the command prompt:

    ```
    mvn test -Dcucumber.options="--tags @sanity --tags
       @regression"
    ```

    This is the output:

```
------------------------------------------------------
T E S T S
------------------------------------------------------
Running com.CucumberOptions.RunCukeTest
@important
Feature: Home Page

  Background: flow till home page           # sample.feature:4
    Given user is on Application home page # LoginSteps.user_is_on_Application_home_page()

  @sanity @regression
  Scenario: Top Banner content             # sample.feature:17
    When user focuses on Top Banner        # LoginSteps.user_focuses_on_Top_Banner()
    Then user gets an option of home page # LoginSteps.user_gets_an_option_of_home_page()

1 Scenarios (1 passed)
3 Steps (3 passed)
0m0.431s

Tests run: 4, Failures: 0, Errors: 0, Skipped: 0, Time elapsed: 1.011 sec
```

Running only one Scenario which is Tagged both @sanity and @regression.

2. If we want to run, the Scenarios which are Tagged either `sanity` or `regression`, then run the following command in the command prompt:

   **`mvn test -Dcucumber.options="--tags @regression,@sanity"`**

   This is the output:

```
Running com.CucumberOptions.RunCukeTest
@important
Feature: Home Page

  Background: flow till home page        # sample.feature:4
    Given user is on Application home page # LoginSteps.user_is_on_Application_home_page()

  @sanity
  Scenario: Home Page Default content       # sample.feature:8
    Then user gets a github bootcamp section # LoginSteps.user_gets_a_github_bootcamp_section()

  Background: flow till home page        # sample.feature:4
    Given user is on Application home page # LoginSteps.user_is_on_Application_home_page()

  @regression
  Scenario: GitHub Bootcamp Section             # sample.feature:12
    When user focuses on GitHub Bootcamp Section # LoginSteps.user_focuses_on_GitHub_Bootcamp_Section()
    Then user gets an option to setup git        # LoginSteps.user_gets_an_option_to_setup_git()

  Background: flow till home page        # sample.feature:4
    Given user is on Application home page # LoginSteps.user_is_on_Application_home_page()

  @sanity @regression
  Scenario: Top Banner content             # sample.feature:17
    When user focuses on Top Banner        # LoginSteps.user_focuses_on_Top_Banner()
    Then user gets an option of home page # LoginSteps.user_gets_an_option_of_home_page()

3 Scenarios (3 passed)
8 Steps (8 passed)
0m0.228s

Tests run: 11, Failures: 0, Errors: 0, Skipped: 0, Time elapsed: 1.078 sec
```

Running the Scenarios that are tagged as either `@sanity` or `@regression`

3. Update the `home_page.feature` file to the following:

   ```
   @important
   Feature: Home Page

       Background: flow till home page
         Given user is on Application home page

       @sanity @wip
       Scenario: Home Page Default content
         Then user gets a GitHub Bootcamp section

       @regression @wip
       Scenario: GitHub Bootcamp Section
   ```

```
       When user focuses on GitHub Bootcamp Section
       Then user gets an option to setup git


    @sanity @regression
    Scenario: Top Banner content
       When user focuses on Top Banner
   Then user gets an option of home page
```

4.  If we want to run the Scenarios which are either Tagged @sanity AND @wip or
    @regression AND @wip, run the following command:

    ```
    mvn test -Dcucumber.options="--tags @sanity,@regression --tags
    @wip"
    ```

    This is the output:

```
-------------------------------------------------
 T E S T S
-------------------------------------------------
Running com.CucumberOptions.RunCukeTest
@important
Feature: Home Page

  Background: flow till home page        # sample.feature:4
    Given user is on Application home page # LoginSteps.user_is_on_Application_home_page()

  @sanity @wip
  Scenario: Home Page Default content      # sample.feature:8
    Then user gets a github bootcamp section # LoginSteps.user_gets_a_github_bootcamp_section()

  Background: flow till home page        # sample.feature:4
    Given user is on Application home page # LoginSteps.user_is_on_Application_home_page()

  @regression @wip
  Scenario: GitHub Bootcamp Section                # sample.feature:12
    When user focuses on GitHub Bootcamp Section # LoginSteps.user_focuses_on_GitHub_Bootcamp_Section()
    Then user gets an option to setup git        # LoginSteps.user_gets_an_option_to_setup_git()

2 Scenarios (2 passed)
5 Steps (5 passed)
0m0.180s

Tests run: 7, Failures: 0, Errors: 0, Skipped: 0, Time elapsed: 0.844 sec
```

## How it works...

Now let's understand why we ANDed and ORed the Tags in the preceding section:

▶   **ANDing**: When we want to run the Scenarios with all the mentioned Tags. Tags
    have to be mentioned in separate --tags options; for example, mvn test
    -Dcucumber.options="--tags @sanity --tags @Regression".

▸ **ORing**: When we want to run the Scenarios with either of the mentioned Tags. Tags have to be mentioned in single –tags options but should be comma separated; for example, mvn test -Dcucumber.options="--tags @wip,@sanity".

 ANDing and ORing can be combined to achieve greater flexibility in achieving what to run.

# Adding Hooks to Cucumber code

After finding out how to run a few selective Features, the next great thing is running some code before or after test Scenarios. These are very basic and desired Features for Test Automation Frameworks. Examples of this could be initializing the browser before the execution starts and closing the browser after the execution is complete. So how do we do this in Cucumber? Let's take a look at this in this recipe.

## Getting ready

For this recipe, we are going to update the home_page.feature file to the one shown as follows:

```
Feature: Home Page

  Background: flow till home page
    Given user is on Application home page

  @sanity @wip
  Scenario: Home Page Default content
    Then user gets a GitHub Bootcamp section

  @regression @wip
  Scenario: GitHub Bootcamp Section
    When user focuses on GitHub Bootcamp Section
    Then user gets an option to setup git
```

## How to do it...

1. In the automation package, create one java class Hooks.java and put the following code in it (focus on the bold and highlighted text):

```
package com.automation;

import org.openqa.selenium.WebDriver;
```

```java
import org.openqa.selenium.firefox.FirefoxDriver;

import cucumber.api.java.After;
import cucumber.api.java.Before;

public class Hooks {

  public static WebDriver driver = null;

  public static String browser = "firefox";
  public static String baseURL = "https://GitHub.com/";

  @Before
  public static void createDriver() {

    System.out.println("Inside Before");
    createDriver(browser);
    OpenURL(baseURL);
  }

  public static void createDriver(final String browserId) {
    if (browserId.equalsIgnoreCase("firefox")) {
      driver = new FirefoxDriver();
    }
  }

  public static void OpenURL(String baseURL) {
    //Maximize window
    driver.manage().window().maximize();

    // Open URL on window
    driver.get(baseURL);
  }

  @After
  public void tearDown() {

    System.out.println("Inside After");
    driver.quit();
  }

}
```

2. Now, run the home_page.feature file from Eclipse itself and note the output:

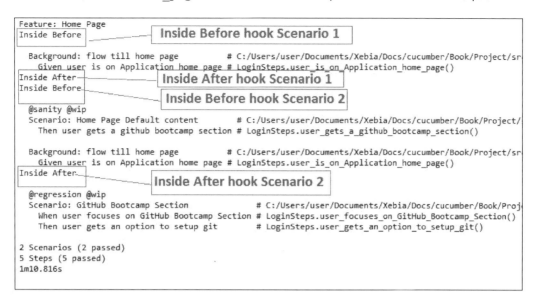

## How it works...

▸ **Hooks**: Cucumber allows us to run a piece of code at certain points in test case execution. This is implemented via Hooks. The real-life use of this involves initializing browsers before execution and closing the browser after execution. The Hooks code is generally kept in a file called Hooks.java, but this is not mandatory.

▸ **@Before**: The Before Hook is run before all the Scenarios of a feature file, including the background. If there are multiple Before Hooks, then they will be run in the order they are written.

▸ **@After**: The After Hook is run after all Scenarios of a feature file. If there are multiple After Hooks, then they will be run in the order they are written.

The following is the order of execution:

1. Before Hook
2. Background
3. Scenario
4. After Hook

## There's more...

Although Hooks are run in the order they are written, the `order` parameter can be used to define custom execution. The default value is `10000`, and Cucumber runs `@Before` Hooks from low to high. A `@Before` Hook with an order of `100` will run before one with an order of `20`. An `@After` Hook runs from high to low—so an `@After` Hook with an order of `200` will run before one with an order of `100`.

Example: `@Before( order=5 )` and `@After( order =20)`

# Tagging the Hooks

What if we want to execute some piece of code only before certain Scenarios and not before all Scenarios? Consider a situation where we want to invoke the Selenium Webdriver for the Scenarios related to browser automation and the `REST` Client code for Scenarios related to `REST` Services automation. How do we do this in Cucumber? Let's see this in the next section.

## Getting ready

For this recipe, we are going to use update `home_page.feature` like this:

```
Feature: Home Page

  Background: flow till home page
    Given user is on Application home page

  @web
  Scenario: Home Page Default content on Web
    Then user gets a GitHub Bootcamp section

  @rest
  Scenario: GitHub account REST Service
    When user sends a GET request
```

## How to do it...

1. Update the code of the `Hooks.java` class with the following code:

   ```java
   package com.automation;

   import org.openqa.selenium.WebDriver;

   import cucumber.api.java.After;
   import cucumber.api.java.Before;
   ```

```java
public class Hooks {

  public static WebDriver driver = null;

  public static String browser = "firefox";
  public static String baseURL = "https://GitHub.com/";

  @Before("@web")
  public static void createDriver() {

    System.out.println("Inside Web Hook");
    //sample code
  }

  @Before("@rest")
  public static void createrestBuilder() {

    System.out.println("Inside REST Hook");
    //sample code
  }

  @After
  public void tearDown() {

    System.out.println("Inside After");
    //Sample Code   }

}
```

2. Run the `home_page.feature` file from Eclipse and save the Cucumber exceptions in the `Step Definitions` file.

3. Run the `home_page.feature` file again from Eclipse; this is the output you will see:

```
Feature: Home Page
Inside Web Hook ........................ Before Hook code for @web

  Background: flow till home page          # C:/Users/user/Documents/Xebia/Docs/cucumber/Book/Project/src/
    Given user is on Application home page # LoginSteps.user_is_on_Application_home_page()
Inside After
Inside rest Hook
                          ———— Before Hook code for @rest
  @web
  Scenario: Home Page Default content on Web # C:/Users/user/Documents/Xebia/Docs/cucumber/Book/Project/sr
    Then user gets a github bootcamp section # LoginSteps.user_gets_a_github_bootcamp_section()

  Background: flow till home page          # C:/Users/user/Documents/Xebia/Docs/cucumber/Book/Project/src/
    Given user is on Application home page # LoginSteps.user_is_on_Application_home_page()
Inside After

  @rest
  Scenario: GitHub account REST Service # C:/Users/user/Documents/Xebia/Docs/cucumber/Book/Project/src/tes
    When user sends a GET request        # LoginSteps.user_sends_a_GET_request()

2 Scenarios (2 passed)
4 Steps (4 passed)
0m0.112s
```

## How it works...

Tagged Hooks are combination of Hooks and Tags. Tagged Hooks are used when we want to perform some action only for specific and not all Scenarios. We have to add the Tag in parentheses after the Hook to transform it into a tagged Hooks.

# ANDing and ORing tagged Hooks

Just as we ANDed and ORed the Tags, same way we can AND and OR the combination of Tags and Hooks. Consider a situation where we need to perform certain Steps for Features, such as for `feature1` and `feature2` but not for other Features. How do we do this in Cucumber? Let's see this in this recipe.

## Getting ready

We will update the `home_page.feature` file like this for this recipe:

```
@important
Feature: Home Page

  Background: flow till home page
    Given user is on Application home page


  @sanity
  Scenario: Home Page Default content
```

```
    Then user gets a GitHub Bootcamp section


@regression
Scenario: GitHub Bootcamp Section
    When user focuses on GitHub Bootcamp Section
    Then user gets an option to setup git


@sanity @regression
Scenario: Top Banner content
    When user focuses on Top Banner
    Then user gets an option of home page
```

## How to Do it

1. To run the Hook code before Scenarios Tagged with `@sanity` or `@regression`, add the following code to the `hooks.java` file:

```
@Before("@sanity,@regression")
public void taggedHookMethod1() {

System.out.println("tagged hook - sanity OR regression");
}
```

2. Run the `feature` file from Eclipse and observe the output:

```
@important
Feature: Home Page
tagged hook - sanity OR regression

  Background: flow till home page          # C:/Users/user/Documents/Xebia/Docs/cucumber/Book/Project/src
    Given user is on Application home page # LoginSteps.user_is_on_Application_home_page()
tagged hook - sanity OR regression

  @sanity
  Scenario: Home Page Default content      # C:/Users/user/Documents/Xebia/Docs/cucumber/Book/Project/s
    Then user gets a github bootcamp section # LoginSteps.user_gets_a_github_bootcamp_section()

  Background: flow till home page          # C:/Users/user/Documents/Xebia/Docs/cucumber/Book/Project/src
    Given user is on Application home page # LoginSteps.user_is_on_Application_home_page()
tagged hook - sanity OR regression

  @regression
  Scenario: GitHub Bootcamp Section                # C:/Users/user/Documents/Xebia/Docs/cucumber/Book/Proje
    When user focuses on GitHub Bootcamp Section # LoginSteps.user_focuses_on_GitHub_Bootcamp_Section()
    Then user gets an option to setup git        # LoginSteps.user_gets_an_option_to_setup_git()

  Background: flow till home page          # C:/Users/user/Documents/Xebia/Docs/cucumber/Book/Project/src
    Given user is on Application home page # LoginSteps.user_is_on_Application_home_page()

  @sanity @regression
  Scenario: Top Banner content             # C:/Users/user/Documents/Xebia/Docs/cucumber/Book/Project/src/
    When user focuses on Top Banner        # LoginSteps.user_focuses_on_Top_Banner()
    Then user gets an option of home page # LoginSteps.user_gets_an_option_of_home_page()

3 Scenarios (3 passed)
8 Steps (8 passed)
0m0.156s
```

The code will be run before all the Scenarios because all Scenarios are either Tagged `@sanity` or `@regression`.

3.  To run Hooks code for the Scenarios Tagged with `@sanity` AND `@regression` both, comment the earlier code in the `Hooks.java` file and add the following code:

```java
@Before({"@sanity","@regression"})
  public void taggedHookMethod2() {

     System.out.println("tagged hook - Sanity AND
Regression");

}
```

4.  Run the `feature` file from Eclipse and observe the output:

```
@important
Feature: Home Page

  Background: flow till home page          # C:/Users/user/Documents/Xebia/Docs/cucumber/Book/Project/sr
    Given user is on Application home page # LoginSteps.user_is_on_Application_home_page()

  @sanity
  Scenario: Home Page Default content        # C:/Users/user/Documents/Xebia/Docs/cucumber/Book/Project/
    Then user gets a github bootcamp section # LoginSteps.user_gets_a_github_bootcamp_section()

  Background: flow till home page          # C:/Users/user/Documents/Xebia/Docs/cucumber/Book/Project/sr
    Given user is on Application home page # LoginSteps.user_is_on_Application_home_page()
tagged hook - Sanity AND Regression

  @regression
  Scenario: GitHub Bootcamp Section                  # C:/Users/user/Documents/Xebia/Docs/cucumber/Book/Proj
    When user focuses on GitHub Bootcamp Section # LoginSteps.user_focuses_on_GitHub_Bootcamp_Section()
    Then user gets an option to setup git        # LoginSteps.user_gets_an_option_to_setup_git()

  Background: flow till home page          # C:/Users/user/Documents/Xebia/Docs/cucumber/Book/Project/sr
    Given user is on Application home page # LoginSteps.user_is_on_Application_home_page()

  @sanity @regression
  Scenario: Top Banner content          # C:/Users/user/Documents/Xebia/Docs/cucumber/Book/Project/src
    When user focuses on Top Banner      # LoginSteps.user_focuses_on_Top_Banner()
    Then user gets an option of home page # LoginSteps.user_gets_an_option_of_home_page()

3 Scenarios (3 passed)
8 Steps (8 passed)
0m0.514s
```

The code will be run before Scenario 3, which has both Tags `@sanity` and `@regression`.

5.  To run the Hooks code for Scenarios Tagged with `@important` but NOT `@regression`, comment the preceding code in the `Hooks.java` file and add the following code to it:

```java
@Before({"@important","~@regression"})
  public void taggedHookMethod3() {
```

```
      System.out.println("Tagged hook- important but NOT
regression");
   }
```

6. Run the `feature` file from Eclipse and observe the output:

```
@important
Feature: Home Page
Tagged hook- important but NOT regression

  Background: flow till home page          # C:/Users/user/Documents/Xebia/Docs/cucumber/Book/Pr
    Given user is on Application home page # LoginSteps.user_is_on_Application_home_page()

  @sanity
  Scenario: Home Page Default content        # C:/Users/user/Documents/Xebia/Docs/cucumber/Book/
    Then user gets a github bootcamp section # LoginSteps.user_gets_a_github_bootcamp_section()

  Background: flow till home page          # C:/Users/user/Documents/Xebia/Docs/cucumber/Book/Pr
    Given user is on Application home page # LoginSteps.user_is_on_Application_home_page()

  @regression
  Scenario: GitHub Bootcamp Section                 # C:/Users/user/Documents/Xebia/Docs/cucumber/B
    When user focuses on GitHub Bootcamp Section # LoginSteps.user_focuses_on_GitHub_Bootcamp_Se
    Then user gets an option to setup git        # LoginSteps.user_gets_an_option_to_setup_git()

  Background: flow till home page          # C:/Users/user/Documents/Xebia/Docs/cucumber/Book/Pr
    Given user is on Application home page # LoginSteps.user_is_on_Application_home_page()

  @sanity @regression
  Scenario: Top Banner content               # C:/Users/user/Documents/Xebia/Docs/cucumber/Book/Pro
    When user focuses on Top Banner        # LoginSteps.user_focuses_on_Top_Banner()
    Then user gets an option of home page # LoginSteps.user_gets_an_option_of_home_page()

3 Scenarios (3 passed)
8 Steps (8 passed)
0m0.290s
```

The code will be run before Scenario 1, which has the @important (by inheritance) and NOT the @regression Tag.

7. To run Hooks code for Scenarios Tagged with (important AND regression OR (important AND wip), comment the earlier code in the Hooks.java file and add the following code to it:

```
@Before({"@important","@regression,@wip"})
public void taggedHookMethod4() {

   System.out.println("Tagged hook -
      (important+regression) OR (important AND wip)");
}
```

8. Run the `feature` file from Eclipse and observe the output:

```
@important
Feature: Home Page

  Background: flow till home page           # C:/Users/user/Documents/Xebia/Docs/cucumber/Book/Project/src
    Given user is on Application home page # LoginSteps.user_is_on_Application_home_page()
  Tagged hook - (important+Rgression) OR (important AND wip)

  @sanity
  Scenario: Home Page Default content        # C:/Users/user/Documents/Xebia/Docs/cucumber/Book/Project/s
    Then user gets a github bootcamp section # LoginSteps.user_gets_a_github_bootcamp_section()

  Background: flow till home page           # C:/Users/user/Documents/Xebia/Docs/cucumber/Book/Project/src
    Given user is on Application home page # LoginSteps.user_is_on_Application_home_page()
  Tagged hook - (important+Rgression) OR (important AND wip)

  @regression
  Scenario: GitHub Bootcamp Section                 # C:/Users/user/Documents/Xebia/Docs/cucumber/Book/Proje
    When user focuses on GitHub Bootcamp Section # LoginSteps.user_focuses_on_GitHub_Bootcamp_Section()
    Then user gets an option to setup git         # LoginSteps.user_gets_an_option_to_setup_git()

  Background: flow till home page           # C:/Users/user/Documents/Xebia/Docs/cucumber/Book/Project/src
    Given user is on Application home page # LoginSteps.user_is_on_Application_home_page()

  @sanity @regression
  Scenario: Top Banner content               # C:/Users/user/Documents/Xebia/Docs/cucumber/Book/Project/src/
    When user focuses on Top Banner         # LoginSteps.user_focuses_on_Top_Banner()
    Then user gets an option of home page # LoginSteps.user_gets_an_option_of_home_page()

3 Scenarios (3 passed)
8 Steps (8 passed)
0m0.155s
```

The code will be run before Scenarios 2 and 3, which have the `@important` (by inheritance) and `@regression` Tags.

## How it works...

Now let's understand the concept of ANDing, ORing, and NOTing the Hooks.

▸ **OR**: The Hooks code will be run when either of the mentioned Tags is associated with the Scenario. Tags are passed in a String and are comma separated. For example:

```
@Before("@sanity,@wip")
```

▸ **AND**: The Hooks code will be run when all the mentioned Tags are associated with the Scenario. Tags are passed as separate Tag Strings. For example:

```
@Before({"@sanity","@regression"})
```

▸ **NOT**: The Hooks code will be run when all of the mentioned Tags are not associated with the Scenario. Tags are passed as separate Tag Strings. For example:

```
@Before({"@important","~@regression"})
```

# 4
# Configuring Cucumber

In this chapter, we will look at the following recipes:

- ▶ Integrating Cucumber with JUnit
- ▶ Overriding the Cucumber Options
- ▶ Running Strict and Running Dry
- ▶ Configuring the Cucumber Console output
- ▶ Directing the Cucumber output to a file
- ▶ Configuring the naming conventions

## Introduction

When we talk about using Cucumber for behavior-driven development, we often talk about Feature files, Scenarios, Background, and Glue Code (Step Definitions). There isn't an iota of doubt that you won't be able to implement Cucumber until you understand the concepts mentioned earlier, but an area that is really important and is very useful in day-to-day Cucumber life is configuring Cucumber.

In this chapter, we will start with integrating Cucumber with JUnit and then start understanding the different configurations that we can do with @CucumberOptions annotation.

## Integrating Cucumber with JUnit

Until now, we have run Cucumber tests either from Eclipse or from a Terminal, but how can we use automation frameworks to work with Cucumber?

How do we integrate Cucumber with JUnit Framework? Let's take a look at this in the next section.

## How to do it...

We need to create a Java class in the `CucumberOptions` package with an empty body and the `@RunWith` annotation. This is how the class should look like:

```
package com.CucumberOptions;

import org.junit.runner.RunWith;
import Cucumber.api.junit.Cucumber;

@RunWith(Cucumber.class)
public class RunCukeTest {
}
```

## How it works...

Cucumber ships with a JUnit runner, `Cucumber.api.junit.Cucumber`. This class tells JUnit to invoke `Cucumber JUnit runner`. It will search for Feature files and run them, providing the output back to JUnit in a format that it understands. Executing this class as any JUnit test class will run all the Features found on the classpath in the same package as this class.

 The name of the `JUnit` class is irrelevant and the class should be empty.

# Overriding the Cucumber Options

Sometimes, depending on the requirements, we would like to override default Cucumber behavior, such as reporting or the project structure, and so on. We can configure Cucumber via the Terminal, but mostly we run Cucumber with JUnit. So how do we configure Cucumber with JUnit Runners, let's see this in our next section.

## How to do it...

1.  Add `@CucumberOptions` to the `RunCuckeTest.java` class and import `Cucumber.api.CucumberOptions`. This is how the updated code for `RunCukeTest.java` should look like:

    ```
    package com.CucumberOptions;

    import org.junit.runner.RunWith;
    import Cucumber.api.CucumberOptions;
    import Cucumber.api.junit.Cucumber;
    ```

```
@RunWith(Cucumber.class)
@CucumberOptions(
//your Cucumber Options code goes here
)
public class RunCukeTest {
}
```

2. Now, let's specify configurations where our Feature files and Step Definitions are located and which Tags are used. This is how the code for `RunCukeTest.java` should look like:

```
package com.CucumberOptions;

import org.junit.runner.RunWith;
import Cucumber.api.CucumberOptions;
import Cucumber.api.junit.Cucumber;

@RunWith(Cucumber.class)
@CucumberOptions(
    Features = "src/test/java/com/Features",
    glue = "com.StepDefinitions",
    Tags = { "~@wip","~@notImplemented","@sanity" }
    )
public class RunCukeTest {
}
```

Refer to the screenshot for more clarity:

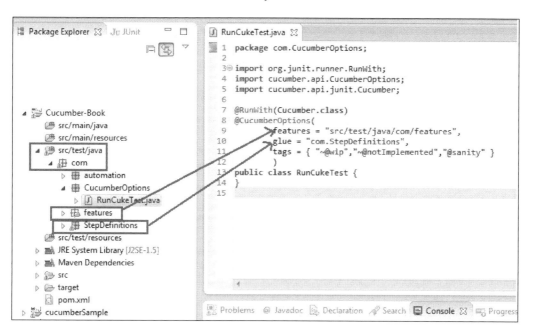

## How it works...

The `@CucumberOptions` annotation provides the same options as the Cucumber Terminal line. For example, we can specify the path to Feature files and to Step Definitions.

The different options that are available are as follows:

| Element | Purpose | Default |
|---|---|---|
| dryRun | true (skips the execution of Glue Code) | FALSE |
| strict | true (will fail execution if there are undefined or pending steps) | FALSE |
| Features | These are the paths to the Feature(s) | {} |
| glue | This declares where to look for Glue Code (Stepdefs and hooks) | {} |
| Tags | This is which Tags in the Features should be executed | {} |
| monochrome | This is whether or not to use monochrome output | FALSE |
| plugin | This declares what formatter(s) to use and also miscellaneous options | {} |

Let's understand the options we have used in this recipe:

- **Features**: This option is used to specify the path to the Feature files. When Cucumber starts execution, it looks for the `.Feature` files at the path/folder mentioned in the **FEATURE** option. Whichever files are with the `.Feature` extension at the path mentioned in the **FEATURE** option, are executed.

- **Glue**: The **GLUE** option is to specify where the Step Definitions and Glue Code are present. Whenever Cucumber encounters a Step, the Cucumber looks for a Step Definition inside all the files present in the folder mentioned in the **GLUE** option. This also holds true for Hooks.

- **Tags**: This option helps you decide which Tags in the Features should be executed or, for that matter, which Tags should not be executed. For example, in our code, whichever Scenario will be Tagged with `@sanity` will be executed and whichever is Tagged with `@wip` will not be executed because of ~ mentioned before the `@wip` Tag. ~ in front of any Tag tells Cucumber to skip the Scenarios/Features tagged with that Tag.

Options that accept multiple values do so in the form of a list. In the preceding table, those Options have been { } marked in the Default column.

# Running Strict and Running Dry

When a Cucumber project becomes big, it becomes very important that we keep the integrity of the system intact. It should not happen that the addition/modification of Scenarios is breaking the system. So, how to quickly check whether all the Steps have an associated Step Definition defined (without executing the code in those Step Definitions)? Let's understand that in our upcoming section.

## How to do it...

1. Add the `dryRun` option to `@CucumberOptions` and set its value to `true`.

2. Add the `strict` option to `@CucumberOptions` and set its value to `false`.

3. Add the `monochrome` option to `@CucumberOptions` and set its value to `true`.

This is how our `RunCukeTest.Java` class should look like:

```
package com.CucumberOptions;

import org.junit.runner.RunWith;
import Cucumber.api.CucumberOptions;
import Cucumber.api.junit.Cucumber;

@RunWith(Cucumber.class)
@CucumberOptions(
    Features = "src/test/java/com/Features",
    glue = "com.StepDefinitions",
    Tags = { "~@wip","~@notImplemented","@sanity" },
    dryRun = true,
    strict = false,
    monochrome = true
    )
public class RunCukeTest {
}
```

## How it works...

Let's understand dryRun, and strict, and Monochrome:

- **dryRun**: If the dryRun option is set to true, Cucumber only checks if all the Steps have their corresponding Step Definitions defined and the code mentioned in the Step Definitions is not executed and vice versa.

  This is used to validate whether we have defined a Step Definition for each Step or not. Consider if someone has added new Scenarios to the project and wants to check whether he has missed any Step Definitions. He assigns true to the dryRun option and runs all Scenarios. Cucumber checks for matching Step Definitions for all Scenarios, without executing the code between Step Definitions, and returns the result. This technique saves a lot of time as compared to Cucumber executing the code in Step Definitions.

- **strict**: If the strict option is set to false, and at execution time if Cucumber encounters any undefined/pending Steps, then Cucumber does not fail the execution and undefined Steps are skipped, and the build is successful. This is what the Console output looks like:

```
1 Scenarios (1 undefined)
3 Steps (1 skipped, 2 undefined)
0m0.000s


You can implement missing steps with the snippets below:

@Given("^user is on search page$")
public void user_is_on_search_page() throws Throwable {
    // Write code here that turns the phrase above into concrete actions
    throw new PendingException();
}

@Then("^user gets an option to create a new creative$")
public void user_gets_an_option_to_create_a_new_creative() throws Throwable {
    // Write code here that turns the phrase above into concrete actions
    throw new PendingException();
}

Tests run: 5, Failures: 0, Errors: 0, Skipped: 4, Time elapsed: 0.507 sec

Results :

Tests run: 5, Failures: 0, Errors: 0, Skipped: 4

[INFO] ------------------------------------------------------------------------
[INFO] BUILD SUCCESS
[INFO] ------------------------------------------------------------------------
```

If Option is set to `true`, and at execution time, if Cucumber encounters any Undefined/Pending Steps, then Cucumber fails the execution and undefined Steps are marked as failure. This is what the Console output looks like:

```
1 Scenarios (1 undefined)
3 Steps (1 skipped, 2 undefined)
0m0.000s


You can implement missing steps with the snippets below:

@Given("^user is on search page$")
public void user_is_on_search_page() throws Throwable {
    // Write code here that turns the phrase above into concrete actions
    throw new PendingException();
}

@Then("^user gets an option to create a new creative$")
public void user_gets_an_option_to_create_a_new_creative() throws Throwable {
    // Write code here that turns the phrase above into concrete actions
    throw new PendingException();
}

Tests run: 5, Failures: 0, Errors: 4, Skipped: 1, Time elapsed: 0.534 sec <<< FAILURE!

Results :

Tests in error:
  Given user is on search page(Scenario: Undefined Steps): TODO: implement me
  Scenario: Undefined Steps: TODO: implement me
  Then user gets an option to create a new creative(Scenario: Undefined Steps): TODO: implement me
  Scenario: Undefined Steps: TODO: implement me

Tests run: 5, Failures: 0, Errors: 4, Skipped: 1

[INFO] ------------------------------------------------------------
[INFO] BUILD FAILURE
[INFO] ------------------------------------------------------------
```

▶ **Monochrome**: If the `monochrome` option is set to `false`, then the console output is not as readable as it should be. The output when the `monochrome` option is set to `false` is shown in the following screenshot:

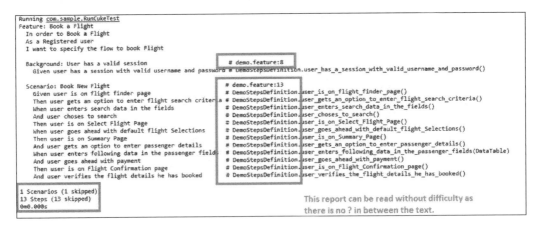

The output when the `monochrome` option is set to `true` is shown in the following screenshot:

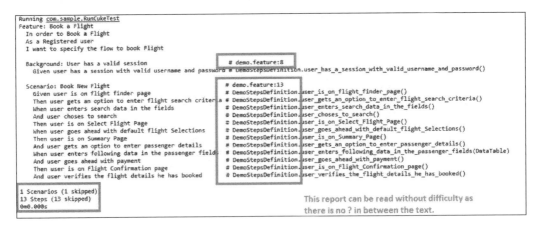

# Configuring the Cucumber Console output

When we execute Cucumber Scenarios, it generates an output to the terminal or the eclipse console. There is a default behavior associated with that output and we can also configure that output as per our needs also. So how do we modify the default behavior, let's see this in the next section.

## How to do it...

1.  Add the `plugin` option to `@CucumberOptions` and set its value to `{ "progress" }`. This is how the `@CucumberOptions` code looks like:

```
@CucumberOptions (
        Features = "src/test/java/com/Features",
        glue = "com.StepDefinitions",
        Tags = { "~@wip","~@notImplemented","@sanity" },
        dryRun = false,
        strict = true,
        monochrome = true,
        plugin = { "progress" }
        )
```

2.  If we run the Scenarios now via the Terminal, this is what our output looks like:

```
---------------------------------------------------------
 T E S T S
---------------------------------------------------------
Running com.CucumberOptions.RunCukeTest
1
.F1              Progress - plugin
.U-

2 Scenarios (1 failed, 1 undefined)
5 Steps (1 failed, 1 skipped, 1 undefined, 2 passed)
0m0.207s
```

3.  Instead of the `progress` plugin, we can also use the `pretty` plugin, which is more verbose as compared to the `progress` plugin. This is what the code looks like:

```
@CucumberOptions (
     Features = "src/test/java/com/Features",
     glue = "com.StepDefinitions",
     Tags = { "~@wip","~@notImplemented","@sanity" },
     dryRun = false,
     strict = true,
```

```
        monochrome = true,
    plugin = { "pretty" }
  )
```

4.  This is what the output looks like:

```
-------------------------------------------------------
 T E S T S
-------------------------------------------------------
Running com.CucumberOptions.RunCukeTest
@important                          These details were missing in
Feature: Home Page
1                                   progress plugin

  @sanity
  Scenario: Home Page Default content       # sample.feature:5
    Given user is on Application home page   # LoginSteps.user_is_on_Application_home_page()
    Then user gets a github bootcamp section # LoginSteps.user_gets_a_github_bootcamp_section()
      junit.framework.AssertionFailedError
        at junit.framework.Assert.fail(Assert.java:55)
        at junit.framework.Assert.assertTrue(Assert.java:22)
        at junit.framework.Assert.assertTrue(Assert.java:31)
        at com.StepDefinitions.LoginSteps.user_gets_a_github_bootcamp_section(LoginSteps.java:158)
        at ?.Then user gets a github bootcamp section(sample.feature:7)
1

  @sanity @regression
  Scenario: Top Banner content              # sample.feature:16
    Given user is on Application home page # LoginSteps.user_is_on_Application_home_page()
    When user focuses on Top Banner
    Then user gets an option of home page  # LoginSteps.user_gets_an_option_of_home_page()

2 Scenarios (1 failed, 1 undefined)
5 Steps (1 failed, 1 skipped, 1 undefined, 2 passed)
0m0.190s
```

5.  If we are more concerned about the time taken by each Step Definition, then we should use the `usage` plugin. This is what the `@CucumberOptions` code looks like:

```
@CucumberOptions (
      Features = "src/test/java/com/Features",
      glue = "com.StepDefinitions",
      Tags = { "~@wip","~@notImplemented","@sanity" },
      dryRun = false,
      strict = true,
      monochrome = true,
      plugin = { "usage" }
      )
```

6. This is what the output looks like:

```
------------------------------------------------------------
TESTS
------------------------------------------------------------
Running com.CucumberOptions.RunCukeTest
1
1
[
  {
    "source": "^user is on Application home page$",
    "steps": [
      {
        "name": "user is on Application home page",
        "aggregatedDurations": {
          "median": 0.139297234,
          "average": 0.139297234
        },
        "durations": [
          {
            "duration": 0.278244292,
            "location": "sample.feature:6"
          },
          {
            "duration": 0.000350176,
            "location": "sample.feature:17"
          }
        ]
      }
    ]
  },
  {
    "source": "^user gets an option of home page$",
    "steps": [
```

Duration

7. If you are expecting some Scenarios to fail, and want to re-run the failed Scenarios, only then use the `Rerun` plugin. This is what the code for `@CucumberOptions` looks like:

```
@CucumberOptions(
    Features = "src/test/java/com/Features",
    glue = "com.StepDefinitions",
    Tags = { "~@wip","~@notImplemented","@sanity" },
    dryRun = false,
    strict = true,
    monochrome = true,
    plugin = { "rerun" }
)
```

8.  This is what the output looks like:

```
--------------------------------------------------
 T E S T S
--------------------------------------------------
Running com.CucumberOptions.RunCukeTest
1
1                        _____failed scenario location
sample.feature:5
2 Scenarios (1 failed, 1 passed)
5 Steps (1 failed, 4 passed)
0m0.221s

junit.framework.AssertionFailedError
        at junit.framework.Assert.fail(Assert.java:55)
        at junit.framework.Assert.assertTrue(Assert.java:22)
        at junit.framework.Assert.assertTrue(Assert.java:31)
        at com.StepDefinitions.LoginSteps.user_gets_a_github_bootcamp_section(LoginSteps.java:158)
        at ?.Then user gets a github bootcamp section(sample.feature:7)

Tests run: 7, Failures: 2, Errors: 0, Skipped: 0, Time elapsed: 0.867 sec <<< FAILURE!
```

## How it works...

Let's understand the different plugins used in the preceding Steps:

▶ **progress**: This is Cucumber's default plugin and produces one character per Step. Each character represents the status of each Step:

  ❑  . means passing

  ❑  U means undefined

  ❑  - means skipped (or a Scenario Outline Step)

  ❑  F means failing

▶ **pretty**: This is a more verbose plugin with information such as which Step matched which Step Definition, arguments and the location of Steps, and so on.

▶ **usage**: This sorts the Step Definitions by their average execution time. The output from the usage plugin is useful for quickly finding slow parts in your code but it is also a great way to get an overview of your Step Definitions.

▶ **rerun**: This plugin outputs the location of failing Scenarios so that these can be directly used in the next execution. If all the Scenarios are passing, then the rerun plugin does not produce anything.

# Directing the Cucumber output to a file

Cucumber integrates business logic with code, so our focus is on business rather than code. The same philosophy is also followed in the Cucumber reports. Cucumber reports are more about business utility rather than to do with more charts.

Robust automation frameworks generate very good and detailed reports, which can be shared with all stake holders. There are multiple options available for reports which can be used depending on the requirement. Let's check out how to use reports extensively in our next section.

## How to do it...

1. For HTML reports, add `html:target/Cucumber` to the `@CucumberOptions` plugin option. This is what the code for `@CucumberOptions` looks like:

```
@CucumberOptions(
        Features = "src/test/java/com/Features",
        glue = "com.StepDefinitions",
        Tags = { "~@wip","~@notImplemented","@sanity" },
        dryRun = false,
        strict = true,
        monochrome = true,
        plugin = { "progress",
                "html:target/Cucumber"
            }
    )
```

2. For JSON reports, add `json:target_json/Cucumber.json` to the `@CucumberOptions` plugin option. This is what the code for `@CucumberOptions` looks like:

```
@CucumberOptions(
        Features = "src/test/java/com/Features",
        glue = "com.StepDefinitions",
        Tags = { "~@wip","~@notImplemented","@sanity" },
        dryRun = false,
        strict = true,
        monochrome = true,
        plugin = { "pretty",
                "json:target_json/Cucumber.json"
            }
    )
```

3. For JUnit reports, add `junit:target_json/Cucumber_junit.xml` to the `@CucumberOptions` plugin option. This is what the code for `@CucumberOptions` looks like:

```
@CucumberOptions(
        Features = "src/test/java/com/Features",
        glue = "com.StepDefinitions",
        Tags = { "~@wip","~@notImplemented","@sanity" },
        dryRun = false,
```

```
        strict = true,
        monochrome = true,
        plugin = { "pretty",
             "junit:target_json/Cucumber_junit.xml"
            }
        )
```

## How it works...

By default, the plugin's output is redirected to STDOUT and if we want to store that output to a file format, we need to redirect the output to that file. The syntax is as follows:

```
FORMAT : <<filepath>>
```

Let's understand each output in detail:

> **HTML**: This will generate an HTML report at the location mentioned in the formatter itself. This is what the HTML file looks like:

▸ **JSON**: This report contains all the information from the gherkin source in the JSON format. This report is meant to be postprocessed into another visual format by third-party tools, such as Cucumber Jenkins. This is what JSON reports look like:

```
1 [
2    {
3       "id": "home-page",
4       "tags": [
5          {
6             "name": "@important",
7             "line": 1
8          }
9       ],
10      "description": "",
11      "name": "Home Page",
12      "keyword": "Feature",
13      "line": 2,
14      "elements": [
15         {
16            "id": "home-page;home-page-default-content",
17            "tags": [
18               {
19                  "name": "@sanity",
20                  "line": 4
21               }
22            ],
23            "description": "",
24            "name": "Home Page Default content",
25            "keyword": "Scenario",
26            "line": 5,
27            "steps": [
28               {
29                  "result": {
30                     "duration": 213511380,
31                     "status": "passed"
32                  },
33                  "name": "user is on Application home page",
34                  "keyword": "Given ",
35                  "line": 6,
```

▸ **JUnit**: This report generates XML files just like Apache Ant's `junitreport` task. This XML format is understood by most continuous integration servers, who will use it to generate visual reports. This is what JUnit reports look like:

```
 1  <?xml version="1.0" encoding="UTF-8"?><testsuite failures="1" name="cucumber.runtime.formatter.JUnitFormatter" skipped="0" tests="2" time="0.160588"
 2  <testcase classname="Home Page" name="Home Page Default content" time="0.16044">
 3  <failure message="junit.framework.AssertionFailedError&#13;&#10;&#9;at junit.framework.Assert.fail(Assert.java:55)&#13;&#10;&#9;at junit.framework.A
 4  Then user gets a github bootcamp section...............................failed
 5
 6  StackTrace:
 7  junit.framework.AssertionFailedError
 8
 9      at junit.framework.Assert.fail(Assert.java:55)                                        Errors
10
11      at junit.framework.Assert.assertTrue(Assert.java:22)
12
13      at junit.framework.Assert.assertTrue(Assert.java:31)
14
15      at com.StepDefinitions.LoginSteps.user_gets_a_github_bootcamp_section(LoginSteps.java:158)
16
17      at ⓪.Then user gets a github bootcamp section(sample.feature:7)
18
19  ]]></failure>
20  </testcase>
21  <testcase classname="Home Page" name="Top Banner content" time="0.000148">
22  <system-out><![CDATA[Given user is on Application home page...................................passed       Steps
23  When user focuses on Top Banner...............................................passed
24  Then user gets an option of home page.........................................passed
25  ]]></system-out>
26  </testcase>
27  </testsuite>
```

# Configuring the naming conventions

As Cucumber can be implemented in multiple languages, developers with multiple language knowledge and background can work on the same project. So, sometimes it might be difficult for teams to manage the naming conventions, such as underscore or camel case.

Cucumber lets the team choose the naming convention. Depending on the naming convention, Cucumber generates the method names for Step Definitions. Let's see how it can be done in the next section.

## How to do it...

1. If you want to use camel case, then add the following code to `@CucumberOptions`:

   ```
   snippets=SnippetType.CAMELCASE
   ```

2. If you want to use underscore, then add the following code to `@CucumberOptions`.

   ```
   snippets=SnippetType.UNDERSCORE
   ```

3. This is what the code for `RunCukeTest.Java` looks like:

   ```
   package com.CucumberOptions;

   import org.junit.runner.RunWith;
   import Cucumber.api.CucumberOptions;
   import Cucumber.api.SnippetType;
   import Cucumber.api.junit.Cucumber;
   ```

```
@RunWith(Cucumber.class)
@CucumberOptions(
    Features = "src/test/java/com/Features",
    glue = "com.StepDefinitions",
    Tags = { "~@wip","~@notImplemented","@sanity" },
    dryRun = false,
    strict = true,
    monochrome = true,
    plugin = { "pretty",
            "junit:target_junit/Cucumber.xml"
        },
    Snippets = SnippetType.CAMELCASE
    )
public class RunCukeTest {
}
```

## How it works...

Let's understand the `Snippets` option in detail:

**Snippets**: This option is typed, so you'll need to use one of the constants provided, that is, `SnippetType.CAMELCASE` or `SnippetType.UNDERSCORE`. Remember to import `Cucumber.api.SnippetType`. The default option is underscore. The Step Definition suggestion if we chose camel case is shown as follows:

```
Running com.CucumberOptions.RunCukeTest
@important
Feature: Home Page

  @sanity
  Scenario: Home Page Default content        # sample.feature:5
    Given user is on Application home page
    Then user gets a github bootcamp section # LoginSteps.user_gets_a_github_bootcamp_section()

  @sanity @regression
  Scenario: Top Banner content               # sample.feature:16
    Given user is on Application home page
    When user focuses on Top Banner          # LoginSteps.user_focuses_on_Top_Banner()
    Then user gets an option of home page    # LoginSteps.user_gets_an_option_of_home_page()

2 Scenarios (2 undefined)
5 Steps (3 skipped, 2 undefined)
0m0.000s


You can implement missing steps with the snippets below:

@Given("^user is on Application home page$")
public void userIsOnApplicationHomePage() throws Throwable {
    // Write code here that turns the phrase above into concrete actions
    throw new PendingException();
}

Tests run: 7, Failures: 0, Errors: 4, Skipped: 3, Time elapsed: 1.044 sec <<< FAILURE!
```

# 5

# Running Cucumber

In this chapter, we will cover the following recipes:

- ▸ Integrating Cucumber with Maven
- ▸ Running Cucumber from the Terminal
- ▸ Overriding options from the Terminal
- ▸ Integrating Cucumber with Jenkins and GitHub
- ▸ Running Cucumber test cases in parallel

## Introduction

For successful implementation of any testing framework, it is mandatory that test cases can be run in multiple ways so that people with different competency levels can use it how they need to. So, now we will focus on running Cucumber test cases. There are multiple ways of running Cucumber, such as integrating it with Maven and running it from the Terminal; we can run Cucumber remotely as well by integrating Cucumber with Jenkins.

In this chapter, we will also cover advanced topics of running Cucumber test cases in parallel by a combination of Cucumber, Maven, and JUnit.

## Integrating Cucumber with Maven

Maven has a lot of advantages over other build tools, such as dependency management, lots of plugins and the convenience of running integration tests. So let's also integrate our framework with Maven. Maven will allow our test cases to be run in different flavors, such as from the Terminal, integrating with Jenkins, and parallel execution.

So how do we integrate with Maven? Let's find out in the next section.

## Getting ready

I am assuming that we know the basics of Maven (the basics of Maven are out of the scope of this book). Follow the upcoming instructions to install Maven on your system and to create a sample Maven project.

1. We need to install Maven on our system first. So, follow instructions mentioned on the following blogs:

   For Windows:

   `http://www.mkyong.com/maven/how-to-install-maven-in-windows/`

   For Mac:

   `http://www.mkyong.com/maven/install-maven-on-mac-osx/`

2. We can also install the Maven Eclipse plugin by following the instructions mentioned on this blog:

   `http://theopentutorials.com/tutorials/eclipse/installing-m2eclipse-maven-plugin-for-eclipse/`.

3. To import a Maven project into Eclipse, follow the instructions on this blog:

   `http://www.tutorialspoint.com/maven/maven_eclispe_ide.htm`.

## How to do it...

Since it is a Maven project, we are going to change the `pom.xml` file to add the Cucumber dependencies.

1. First we are going to declare some custom properties which will be used by us in managing the dependency version:

```xml
<properties>
    <junit.version>4.11</junit.version>
    <cucumber.version>1.2.2</cucumber.version>
    <selenium.version>2.45.0</selenium.version>
    <maven.compiler.version>2.3.2</maven.compiler.version>
</properties>
```

2. Now, we are going to add the dependency for Cucumber-JVM with scope as test:

```xml
<!-- Cucumber-java-->
  <dependency>
    <groupId>info.cukes</groupId>
    <artifactId>cucumber-java</artifactId>
    <version>${cucumber.version}</version>
    <scope>test</scope>
  </dependency>
```

3. Now we need to add the dependency for Cucumber-JUnit with scope as test.

```
<!-- Cucumber-JUnit -->
  <dependency>
    <groupId>info.cukes</groupId>
    <artifactId>cucumber-junit</artifactId>
    <version>${cucumber.version}</version>
    <scope>test</scope>
  </dependency>
```

That's it! We have integrated Cucumber and Maven.

## How it works...

By following these Steps, we have created a Maven project and added the Cucumber-Java dependency. At the moment, this project only has a `pom.xml` file, but this project can be used for adding different modules such as Feature files and Step Definitions.

The advantage of using properties is that we are making sure that the dependency version is declared at one place in the `pom.xml` file. Otherwise, we declare a dependency at multiple places and may end up with a discrepancy in the dependency version.

The Cucumber-Java dependency is the main dependency necessary for the different building blocks of Cucumber. The **Cucumber-JUnit** dependency is for Cucumber JUnit Runner, which we use in running Cucumber test cases.

# Running Cucumber from the Terminal

Now we have integrated Cucumber with Maven, running Cucumber from the Terminal will not be a problem. Running any test framework from the Terminal has its own advantages, such as overriding the run configurations mentioned in the code.

So how do we run Cucumber test cases from the Terminal? Let's find out in our next section.

## How to do it...

1. Open the command prompt and `cd` until the project root directory.

2. First, let's run all the Cucumber Scenarios from the command prompt. Since it's a Maven project and we have added Cucumber in test scope dependency and all features are also added in test packages, run the following command in the command prompt:

   `mvn test`

This is the output:

```
CMD Command Prompt

C:\Users\user\Documents\Xebia\Docs\cucumber\Book\Project\CucumberBook>mvn test
[INFO] Scanning for projects...
[INFO]
[INFO] Using the builder org.apache.maven.lifecycle.internal.builder.singlethreaded.SingleThreadedBuilder with a thread count of 1
[INFO]
[INFO] ------------------------------------------------------------------------
[INFO] Building Cucumber-Book 0.0.1-SNAPSHOT
[INFO] ------------------------------------------------------------------------
[INFO]
[INFO] --- maven-resources-plugin:2.6:resources (default-resources) @ Cucumber-Book ---
[WARNING] Using platform encoding (Cp1252 actually) to copy filtered resources, i.e. build is platform dependent!
[INFO] Copying 0 resource
[INFO]
[INFO] --- maven-compiler-plugin:2.5.1:compile (default-compile) @ Cucumber-Book ---
[INFO] Nothing to compile - all classes are up to date
[INFO]
[INFO] --- maven-resources-plugin:2.6:testResources (default-testResources) @ Cucumber-Book ---
[WARNING] Using platform encoding (Cp1252 actually) to copy filtered resources, i.e. build is platform dependent!
[INFO] Copying 0 resource
[INFO]
[INFO] --- maven-compiler-plugin:2.5.1:testCompile (default-testCompile) @ Cucumber-Book ---
[WARNING] File encoding has not been set, using platform encoding Cp1252, i.e. build is platform dependent!
[INFO] Compiling 1 source file to C:\Users\user\Documents\Xebia\Docs\cucumber\Book\Project\CucumberBook\target\test-classes
[INFO]
[INFO] --- maven-surefire-plugin:2.12.4:test (default-test) @ Cucumber-Book ---
[INFO] Surefire report directory: C:\Users\user\Documents\Xebia\Docs\cucumber\Book\Project\CucumberBook\target\surefire-reports

 T E S T S
-------------------------------------------------
Running com.CucumberOptions.RunCukeTest            ────→ Running the junit runner class
# language: da
Egenskab: prøve ansøgning
    For at teste login side
```

```
  @regression
  Scenario: GitHub Bootcamp Section            # sample.feature:10
    Given user is on Application home page     # LoginSteps.user_is_on_Application_home_page()
    When user focuses on GitHub Bootcamp Section # LoginSteps.user_focuses_on_GitHub_Bootcamp_Section()
    Then user gets an option to setup git      # LoginSteps.user_gets_an_option_to_setup_git()

  # @sanity @regression
  Scenario: Top Banner content                 # sample.feature:16
    Given user is on Application home page # LoginSteps.user_is_on_Application_home_page()
    When user focuses on Top Banner            # LoginSteps.user_focuses_on_Top_Banner()
    Then user gets an option of home page  # LoginSteps.user_gets_an_option_of_home_page()

14 Scenarios (14 passed)
72 Steps (72 passed)
0m0.261s

Tests run: 86, Failures: 0, Errors: 0, Skipped: 0, Time elapsed: 1.489 sec

Results :

Tests run: 86, Failures: 0, Errors: 0, Skipped: 0

[INFO] ------------------------------------------------------------------------
[INFO] BUILD SUCCESS
[INFO] ------------------------------------------------------------------------
[INFO] Total time: 4.759 s
[INFO] Finished at: 2015-03-29T11:27:01+05:30
[INFO] Final Memory: 15M/166M
[INFO] ------------------------------------------------------------------------
C:\Users\user\Documents\Xebia\Docs\cucumber\Book\Project\CucumberBook>
```

3. The previous command runs everything as mentioned in the JUnit Runner class. However, if we want to override the configurations mentioned in the Runner, then we need to use following command:

   ```
   mvn test -DCucumber.options="<<OPTIONS>>"
   ```

4. If you need help on these Cucumber options, then enter the following command in the command prompt and look at the output:

   ```
   mvn test -Dcucumber.options="--help"
   ```

   This is the output:

```
T E S T S
-------------------------------------------------------
Running com.CucumberOptions.RunCukeTest
Usage: java cucumber.api.cli.Main [options] [[[FILE|DIR][:LINE[:LINE]*] ]+ | @FILE ]

Options:     options                                    descriptions

  -g, --glue PATH                         Where glue code (step definitions and hooks) is loaded from.
  -p, --plugin PLUGIN[:PATH_OR_URL]       Register a plugin.
                                          Built-in PLUGIN types: junit, html, pretty, progress, json, usage,
                                          rerun. PLUGIN can also be a fully qualified class name, allowing
                                          registration of 3rd party plugins.
  -f, --format FORMAT[:PATH_OR_URL]       Deprecated. Use --plugin instead.
  -t, --tags TAG_EXPRESSION               Only run scenarios tagged with tags matching TAG_EXPRESSION.
  -n, --name REGEXP                       Only run scenarios whose names match REGEXP.
  -d, --[no-]-dry-run                     Skip execution of glue code.
  -m, --[no-]-monochrome                  Don't colour terminal output.
  -s, --[no-]-strict                      Treat undefined and pending steps as errors.
      --snippets [underscore|camelcase]   Naming convention for generated snippets. Defaults to underscore.
  -v, --version                           Print version.
  -h, --help                              You're looking at it.
  --i18n LANG                             List keywords for in a particular language
                                          Run with "--i18n help" to see all languages

Feature path examples:
  <path>                                  Load the files with the extension ".feature" for the directory <path>
                                          and its sub directories.
  <path>/<name>.feature                   Load the feature file <path>/<name>.feature from the file system.
  classpath:<path>/<name>.feature         Load the feature file <path>/<name>.feature from the classpath.
  <path>/<name>.feature:3:9               Load the scenarios on line 3 and line 9 in the file
                                          <path>/<name>.feature.
  @<path>/<file>                          Parse <path>/<file> for feature paths generated by the rerun formatter.

Results :

Tests run: 0, Failures: 0, Errors: 0, Skipped: 0
```

## How it works...

`mvn test` runs Cucumber Features using Cucumber's JUnit Runner. The `@RunWith` `(Cucumber.class)` annotation on the `RunCukesTest` class tells JUnit to kick off Cucumber. The Cucumber runtime parses the command-line options to know what Feature to run, where the Glue Code lives, what plugins to use, and so on. When you use the JUnit Runner, these options are generated from the `@CucumberOptions` annotation on your test.

# Overriding Options from the Terminal

When it is necessary to override the options mentioned in the JUnit Runner, then we need
`Dcucumber.options` from the Terminal. Let's look at some of the practical examples.

## How to do it...

1. If we want to run a Scenario by specifying the filesystem path, run the following
   command and look at the output:

   ```
   mvn test -Dcucumber.options=
       "src/test/java/com/features/sample.feature:5"
   ```

```
-------------------------------------------------------
 T E S T S
-------------------------------------------------------
Running com.CucumberOptions.RunCukeTest
@important
Feature: sample                      scenario ran from command line

  @sanity
  Scenario: Home Page Default content   # src/test/java/com/features/sample.feature:5
    Given user is on Application home page   # LoginSteps.user_is_on_Application_home_page()
    Then user gets a github bootcamp section # LoginSteps.user_gets_a_github_bootcamp_section()

1 Scenarios (1 passed)
2 Steps (2 passed)
0m0.221s

Tests run: 3, Failures: 0, Errors: 0, Skipped: 0, Time elapsed: 1.047 sec

Results :

Tests run: 3, Failures: 0, Errors: 0, Skipped: 0

[INFO] -------------------------------------------------------------
[INFO] BUILD SUCCESS
[INFO] -------------------------------------------------------------
[INFO] Total time: 3.554 s
[INFO] Finished at: 2015-03-29T12:20:02+05:30
[INFO] Final Memory: 11M/164M
[INFO] -------------------------------------------------------------
C:\Users\user\Documents\Xebia\Docs\cucumber\Book\Project\CucumberBook>█
```

In the preceding code, "5" is the Feature file line number where a Scenario starts.

2. If we want to run the test cases using Tags, then we run the following command and
   notice the output:

   ```
   mvn test -Dcucumber.options="--tags @sanity"
   ```

   The following is the output of the preceding command:

```
----------------------------------------------------------
 T E S T S
----------------------------------------------------------
Running com.CucumberOptions.RunCukeTest
@important
Feature: sample
                             ---- Tag that we ran from command line
  @sanity
  Scenario: Home Page Default content       # sample.feature:5
    Given user is on Application home page  # LoginSteps.user_is_on_Application_home_page()
    Then user gets a github bootcamp section # LoginSteps.user_gets_a_github_bootcamp_section()

1 Scenarios (1 passed)
2 Steps (2 passed)
0m0.197s

Tests run: 3, Failures: 0, Errors: 0, Skipped: 0, Time elapsed: 1.084 sec

Results :

Tests run: 3, Failures: 0, Errors: 0, Skipped: 0

[INFO] ------------------------------------------------------------
[INFO] BUILD SUCCESS
[INFO] ------------------------------------------------------------
[INFO] Total time: 3.680 s
[INFO] Finished at: 2015-03-29T12:25:09+05:30
[INFO] Final Memory: 11M/164M
[INFO] ------------------------------------------------------------
```

3. If we want to generate a different report, then we can use the following command and see the JUnit report generate at the location mentioned:

```
mvn test -Dcucumber.options=
    "--plugin junit:target/cucumber-junit-report.xml"
```

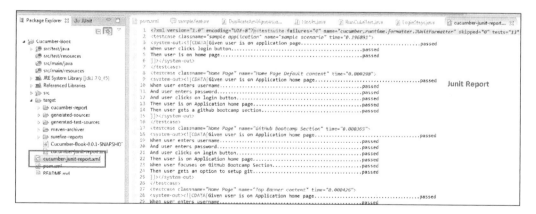

## How it works...

When you override the options with `-Dcucumber.options`, you will completely override whatever options are hardcoded in your `@CucumberOptions`. There is one exception to this rule, and that is the `--plugin` option. This will not override, but instead, it will add a plugin.

# Integrating Cucumber with Jenkins and GitHub

To schedule test case executions remotely, we integrate our testing frameworks with Jenkins. Jenkins has a lot of advantages as it is open source, free, easy to use, can schedule a run on scheduled time or trigger builds after an event, and so on. So it becomes very important that our Cucumber test cases are also run from Jenkins. We will look at this in detail in the next chapter.

## Getting ready

1. Installing and running Jenkins on a local machine is out of the scope of this book. I am assuming that you have either local or remote Jenkins setup ready and can access Jenkins via the URL. If you need any help regarding the setup, follow the Step mentioned in the blog at `https://wiki.jenkins-ci.org/display/JENKINS/Installing+Jenkins`.

2. We will also need to upload our project on GitHub. Again, committing the project on GitHub is out of the scope of this book, but if you need any help, you can follow the instructions mentioned at `https://help.github.com/articles/set-up-git/`

3. The GitHub project URL is `https://github.com/ShankarGarg/CucumberBook.git`, which can be used to download the project we have been using until now.

## How to do it...

1. Open Jenkins in any browser with the URL `http://localhost:8080/jenkins/` (replace localhost with the machine's IP address, if you don't have Jenkins running locally).

2. Go to the Jenkins dashboard and click on **New Item**:

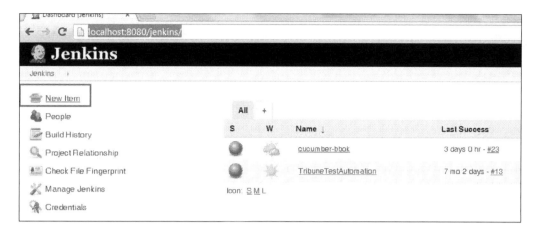

3. Enter the name of the Job that we want to create and also select the **Build a maven project** option. Click on **OK**.

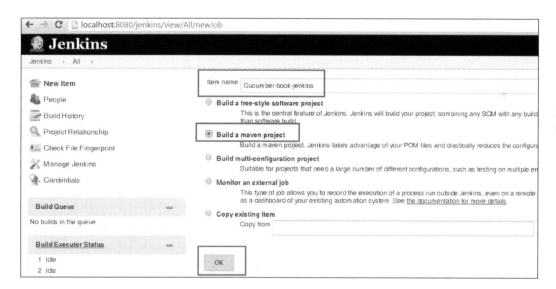

4. Now, enter the **Description** of the project:

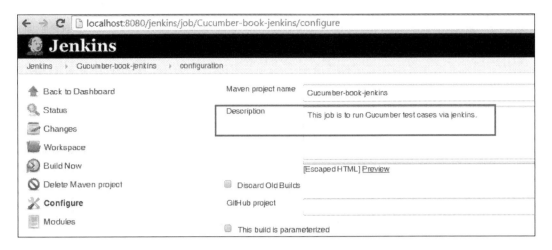

5. Then, enter the Git details by selecting the **Git** option in **Source Code Management** and enter **Repository URL** as `https://github.com/ShankarGarg/CucumberBook.git` and **Credentials**. Keep the other options in this section as default.

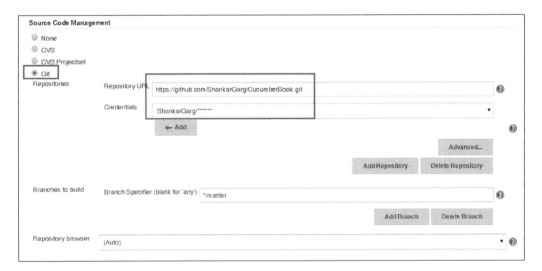

6. Now, we come to the **Build** section. Since we have selected a Maven project, the `Root POM` is automatically mentioned. We need to mention the goal that we want to run, which, in our case, is `test`:

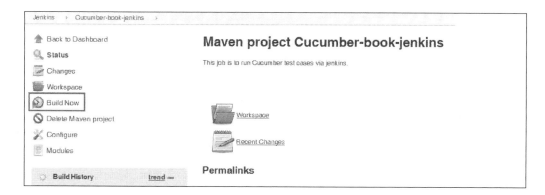

7. Keep all other options as default and click on **Save**.

8. Now, click on **Build Now** to run the project.

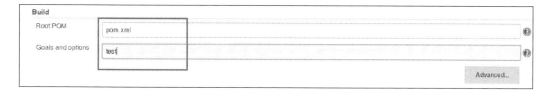

9. Once you click on **Build Now**, a build is triggered immediately. You can see the build number and the timestamp.

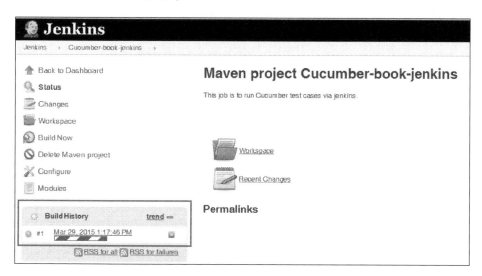

10. Click on the timestamp on the build. And then click on **Console Output**. Just verifying the output to make sure whether the test cases were run or not:

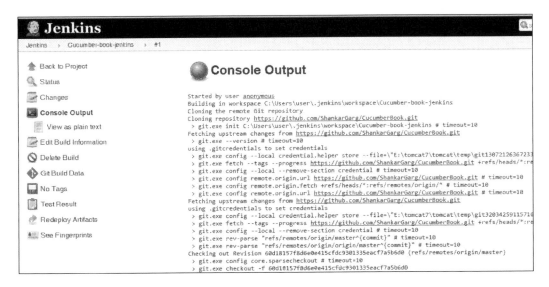

## How it works...

Since we have integrated Maven with Cucumber, the integration with Jenkins was basically running a Maven project with Jenkins. Jenkins comes with a Maven plugin by default (when we selected the item type to **Build a maven project** most of the settings were taken care of at that time) The Build section was prepopulated with pom.xml and we just had to mention the goal as test.

Jenkins is also prepopulated with the GitHub plugin and we just had to mention the GitHub URL and credentials. So now every time the project is built, Jenkins takes the latest code from GitHub and then runs the test cases.

# Running Cucumber test cases in parallel

Running test cases in parallel is a very common and required practice for a good automation framework. Cucumber, by default, does not have any such option or setting. However, since Cucumber can be integrated with Maven and JUnit, using these two tools, we can run Cucumber Scenarios in parallel.

In this recipe, we will run two Scenarios in parallel and, for web automation that will mean opening two browsers at the same time. So how do we make this possible? Let's understand in the next section.

## How to do it...

1. We create a Feature file that has two Scenarios. We will aim to run these two Scenarios in parallel. This is just for the purpose of a demo, you can implement the same approach for *n* number of Scenarios.

   Both the Scenarios will be associated with two different Tags so that they can be run using these tags. Focus on the highlighted tags in the following code; our Feature file should look something like this:

```
Feature: sample

  @sanity
  Scenario: Home Page Default content
     Given user is on Application home page
     Then user gets a GitHub bootcamp section

  @regression
  Scenario: GitHub Bootcamp Section
     Given user is on Application home page
     When user focuses on GitHub Bootcamp Section
     Then user gets an option to setup git
```

2. Now, we should also have Step Definitions ready for this feature file. To focus on the main objective of this recipe, I have kept the code inside Step Definitions as a dummy. Here is what our Step Definition will look like:

```
@Given("^user is on Application home page$")
   public void user_is_on_Application_home_page()  {

      System.out.println("application home");
   }


@Then("^user gets a GitHub bootcamp section$")
   public void user_gets_a_ GitHub_bootcamp_section()  {

      System.out.println("bootcamp section");
   }


@When("^user focuses on GitHub Bootcamp Section$")
   public void user_focuses_on_GitHub_Bootcamp_Section()  {

      System.out.println("focus on GitHub");

   }
```

```
@Then("^user gets an option to setup git$")
  public void user_gets_an_option_to_setup_git() {

    System.out.println("git section");
  }
```

3. The next Step is to write the Runners, which will make sure that test cases run in parallel. The first Step in that direction is to have one `RunCukeTest.java` class, which will specifically run Scenarios associated with the `@sanity` Tag. The code for `RunCukeTest` will be as follows:

```
package com.CucumberOptions;

import org.junit.runner.RunWith;

import cucumber.api.CucumberOptions;
import cucumber.api.junit.Cucumber;

@RunWith(Cucumber.class)
@CucumberOptions(
    features = "src/test/java/com/features",
    glue = "com.StepDefinitions",
    tags = { "@sanity" },
    dryRun = false,
    strict = true,
    monochrome = true,
    plugin = { "pretty",
      "html:target/cucumber_sanity.html"
      }
    )
public class RunCukeTest {
}
```

4. Now we need to write one more Runner, which will run Scenarios tagged with `@regression`. Focus on the highlighted code; the code for `RunCukeParallelTest.java` will look like this:

```
package com.CucumberOptions;

import org.junit.runner.RunWith;

import cucumber.api.CucumberOptions;
import cucumber.api.junit.Cucumber;

@RunWith(Cucumber.class)
@CucumberOptions(
```

```
        features = "src/test/java/com/features",
        glue = "com.StepDefinitions",
        tags = { "@regression" },
        dryRun = false,
        strict = true,
        monochrome=true,
        plugin = { "pretty",
          "html:target/cucumber_regression.html"
        }
        )
public class RunCukeParallelTest {
}
```

5. The last Step is to make sure that these two Runner classes are run in parallel. We will achieve this by making some changes to the pom.xml file. We will add the configuration for the Maven Surefire plugin, which will run the Runner classes in parallel. Here is what we will add to the existing pom.xml file:

```xml
<build>
  <plugins>
    <plugin>
      <groupId>org.apache.maven.plugins</groupId>
      <artifactId>maven-compiler-plugin</artifactId>
      <version>2.5.1</version>
      <configuration>
        <encoding>UTF-8</encoding>
        <source>1.7</source>
        <target>1.7</target>
      </configuration>
    </plugin>
    <plugin>
    <groupId>org.apache.maven.plugins</groupId>
    <artifactId>maven-surefire-plugin</artifactId>
    <version>2.14</version>
    <configuration>
      <skip>true</skip>
    </configuration>
      <executions>
        <execution>
        <id>acceptance-test</id>
        <phase>integration-test</phase>
        <goals>
          <goal>test</goal>
        </goals>
        <configuration>
```

```
            <skip>false</skip>
            <forkCount>2</forkCount>
            <reuseForks>false</reuseForks>
            <argLine>-Duser.language=en</argLine>
            <argLine>-Xmx1024m</argLine>
            <argLine>-XX:MaxPermSize=256m</argLine>
            <argLine>-Dfile.encoding=UTF-8</argLine>
            <useFile>false</useFile>
            <includes>
               <include>**/*Test.class</include>
            </includes>
            <testFailureIgnore>true</testFailureIgnore>
          </configuration>
          </execution>
        </executions>
      </plugin>
    </plugins>
  </build>
```

6. We will also add the dependencies for Selenium, so that we can write the code for invoking the Selenium Webdriver instance. The code for this is as follows:

```
<!-- Selenium -->
<dependency>
    <groupId>org.seleniumhq.selenium</groupId>
    <artifactId>selenium-firefox-driver</artifactId>
    <version>${selenium.version}</version>
</dependency>
<dependency>
    <groupId>org.seleniumhq.selenium</groupId>
    <artifactId>selenium-support</artifactId>
    <version>${selenium.version}</version>
</dependency>
```

7. We will create one more class `DriverFactory.java` for adding Selenium Code, which will have a function to invoke the Firefox browser. The class will look like this:

```
package com.cucumber.automation.utils;

import java.net.MalformedURLException;
import java.util.concurrent.TimeUnit;

import org.openqa.selenium.WebDriver;
import org.openqa.selenium.firefox.FirefoxDriver;
import org.openqa.selenium.support.ui.WebDriverWait;
```

```java
public class DriverFactory {

  public static WebDriver driver = null;
  public static WebDriverWait waitVar = null;

  public static String baseURL = "https://github.com/";

  /**
   *  This function is to invoke Selenium Webdriver
   *
   * @throws MalformedURLException
   * @throws InterruptedException
   */
  public void createDriver() throws MalformedURLException,
    InterruptedException {

    driver = new FirefoxDriver();

    driver.manage().window().maximize();
    driver.manage().timeouts().implicitlyWait(15,
      TimeUnit.SECONDS);

    driver.get(baseURL);

    waitVar = new WebDriverWait(driver, 15);
  }

  /**
   * This function is to close driver instance
   */
  public void teardown() {
    driver.quit();
  }
}
```

8. We will update the `hooks.java` file to add the `createDriver()` function so that Firefox will be invoked before each Scenario. This is how the code will look:

```java
@Before
public void taggedHookMethod1() throws InterruptedException
{
  System.out.println("inside hook");
  DriverFactory.createDriver();
}
```

9. Open Terminal and `cd` until the project root directory. To invoke the Maven configuration that we put in `pom.xml` file, run the following command:

```
mvn integration-test
```

This is the output of the preceding command:

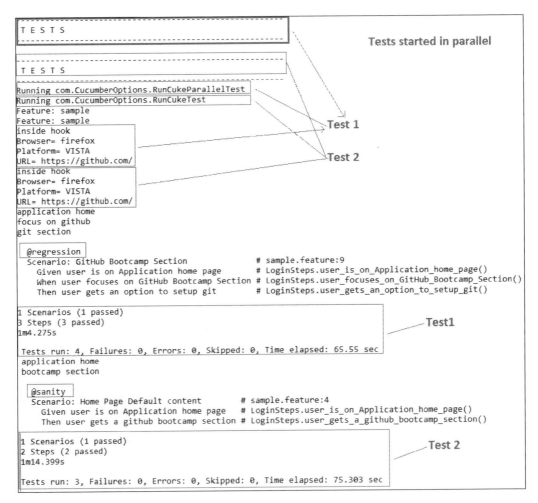

# How it works...

The Maven surefire plugin will run the classes mentioned in the `include` Tag in the configuration Tag as per the `forkcount` Tag value. So all the Java classes that end in `Test` (which are our `RunCukeTest` and `RunCukeParallelTest` JUnit Runner classes) will be executed in parallel in different threads. And since these two classes are JUnit Runner classes, they invoke the execution of Scenarios that are tagged with `@sanity` and on the different thread execution of Scenarios tagged with `@regression`.

# 6
# Building Cucumber Frameworks

In this chapter, we will cover the following recipes:

- ▸ Building a Web Automation framework
- ▸ Building a Mobile Automation framework
- ▸ Building a REST Automation framework

## Introduction

Cucumber is a platform to implement BDD and not automate applications. For automating applications, different APIs are available like Selenium Webdriver for the Web, Appium for mobile, and HTTP Client for REST Services. Until now, we have learned various Cucumber Features so that we can build a robust automation framework but we also need to integrate Cucumber with the APIs mentioned earlier so that we can have frameworks which automate real-time applications.

In this chapter, we will learn how to build frameworks to automate Web, REST, and Mobile applications.

# Building a Web Automation framework

**Selenium** is a Web Automation tool that has made life a lot easier for testers because of its capabilities and powers, and is the number one choice for testers to automate websites. That's the reason we have also chosen Selenium for our framework.

When we create a framework, we should keep in mind that adding new test cases and making changes to existing test cases should be fairly easy and simple.

Let's learn how we can create a robust Web Automation framework using Cucumber and Selenium, along with keeping maintainability and scalability in mind.

## Getting ready

Install Firefox on your system as per the version supported by the latest Selenium version. For more information on Selenium and browser support, visit the web page at `http://docs.seleniumhq.org/about/platforms.jsp`.

## How to do it...

Let's first understand the test case that we will use in this framework. We will test the login functionality of `https://github.com/`. The following is the test case flow:

1. We open `https://github.com/` and click on **Sign in**.

2. We don't enter the username and password and click on **Sign in**:

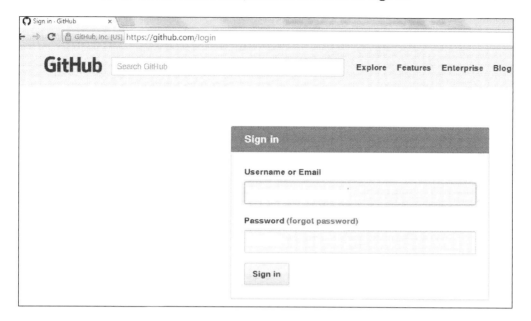

3. We verify the error message we get:

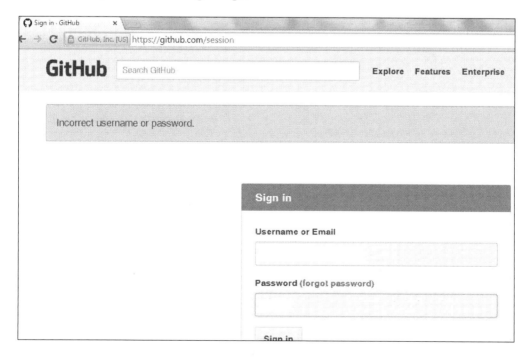

4. We will create a simple Maven project using the Eclipse Maven plugin. Click on **New** in the Eclipse menu and follow the screenshots to create the Maven project named `CucumberWebAutomation`:

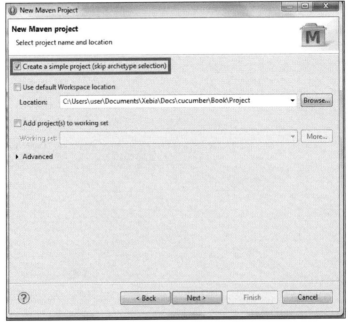

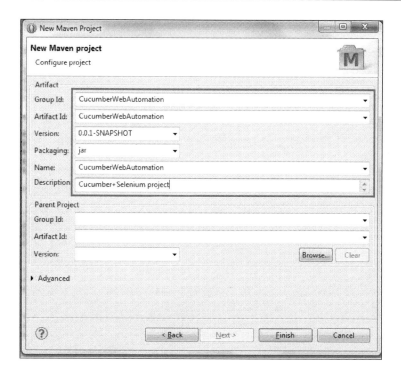

5. Since it is a Maven project, we will update the `pom.xml` file for adding the dependencies of Cucumber and Selenium. As of now, this is what `pom.xml` looks like:

```
<project xmlns="http://maven.apache.org/POM/4.0.0"
  xmlns:xsi="http://www.w3.org/2001/XMLSchema-instance"
   xsi:schemaLocation="http://maven.apache.org/POM/4.0.0
      http://maven.apache.org/xsd/maven-4.0.0.xsd">
  <modelVersion>4.0.0</modelVersion>
  <groupId>CucumberWebAutomation</groupId>
  <artifactId>CucumberWebAutomation</artifactId>
  <version>0.0.1-SNAPSHOT</version>
  <name>CucumberWebAutomation</name>
  <description>Cucumber+Selenium project</description>
</project>
```

6. We will add the `properties` tag and define properties for the Cucumber and Selenium versions so that when we need to update the dependency version, we will need to do it only at one place. Add the following code to `pom.xml` inside the `<project>` tag:

```
<properties>
  <selenium.version>2.45.0</selenium.version>
  <cucumber.version>1.2.2</cucumber.version>
</properties>
```

To check latest dependency version on Maven central repository, refer to `http://search.maven.org/`.

7. We will add dependency for Cucumber-JVM for BDD and Selenium-JVM for web automation. Please add the following code to `pom.xml` after the `</properties>` tag:

```xml
<dependencies>
  <!-- cucumber -->
  <dependency>
    <groupId>info.cukes</groupId>
    <artifactId>cucumber-java</artifactId>
    <version>${cucumber.version}</version>
    <scope>test</scope>
  </dependency>
  <dependency>
    <groupId>info.cukes</groupId>
    <artifactId>cucumber-junit</artifactId>
    <version>${cucumber.version}</version>
    <scope>test</scope>
  </dependency>

  <!-- Selenium -->
  <dependency>
    <groupId>org.seleniumhq.selenium</groupId>
    <artifactId>selenium-java</artifactId>
    <version>${selenium.version}</version>
  </dependency>
</dependencies>
```

8. We will create the project structure and will keep similar files in the same package. Follow the steps shown in this screenshot and create the packages as mentioned:

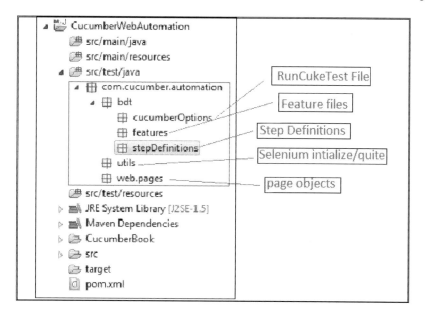

9. Since it is a Cucumber project, we are going to add the `RunCukeTest.java` file to specify the configuration, such as the location of Feature files, the location of Step Definitions, the output location, and so on. Add the following class to the `CucumberOptions` package:

```java
package com.cucumber.automation.bdt.cucumberOptions;

import org.junit.runner.RunWith;

import cucumber.api.CucumberOptions;
import cucumber.api.junit.Cucumber;

@RunWith(Cucumber.class)
@CucumberOptions(

  features =
  "src/test/java/com/cucumber/automation/bdt/features",
    glue = "com.cucumber.automation.bdt.stepDefinitions",
      plugin = {
        "pretty",
          "html:target/cucumber",
  }
)
public class RunCukeTest {
}
```

10. Now it's time to add a Feature file to specify the requirements. We will add the `github_login.feature` file to the package features. This is how our Feature file look likes:

```
Feature: login Page
  In order to test login page
  As a Registered user
  I want to specify the login conditions

  Scenario: login without username and password
    Given user is on github homepage
    When user clicks on Sign in button
    Then user is displayed login screen
    When user clicks Sign in button
    Then user gets an error message "Incorrect username or
      password."
```

11. The next step is to add Step Definitions. The simplest way would be to run the project once and use the suggestions given by Cucumber. Add a `GithubLoginSD.java` file to the `stepDefinitions` package and it should have the following code:

```
package com.cucumber.automation.bdt.stepDefinitions;

import cucumber.api.java.en.Given;
import cucumber.api.java.en.Then;
import cucumber.api.java.en.When;

public class GithubLoginSD {

  @Given("^user is on github homepage$")
  public void user_is_on_github_homepage()  {

  }

  @When("^user clicks on Sign in button$")
  public void user_clicks_on_Sign_in_button()  {

  }

  @Then("^user is displayed login screen$")
  public void user_is_displayed_login_screen()  {

  }

  @When("^user clicks Sign in button$")
  public void user_clicks_Sign_in_button()  {
```

```
    }

    @Then("^user gets an error message \"(.*?)\"$")
    public void user_gets_an_error_message(String arg1)  {


    }


}
```

12. Now we need to add Selenium functions, which can be used to invoke the Firefox browser and close the browser once the execution finishes. I am keeping this file very basic for simplicity purposes. Create the `DriverFactory.java` class in the `utils` package, and the code should look like this:

```
package com.cucumber.automation.utils;

import java.net.MalformedURLException;
import java.util.concurrent.TimeUnit;

import org.openqa.selenium.WebDriver;
import org.openqa.selenium.firefox.FirefoxDriver;
import org.openqa.selenium.support.ui.WebDriverWait;


public class DriverFactory {

    public static WebDriver driver = null;
    public static WebDriverWait waitVar = null;

    public static String baseURL = "https://github.com/";

    /**
     *   This function is to invoke Selenium Webdriver
     *
     * @throws MalformedURLException
     * @throws InterruptedException
     */
    public void createDriver() throws MalformedURLException,
    InterruptedException {

      driver = new FirefoxDriver();

      driver.manage().window().maximize();
```

```
    driver.manage().timeouts().implicitlyWait(15,
      TimeUnit.SECONDS);

    driver.get(baseURL);

    waitVar = new WebDriverWait(driver, 15);
  }

  /**
   * This function is to close driver instance
   */
  public void teardown() {
    driver.quit();
  }
}
```

13. Now we need to hook this code so that the browser can be initiated before each scenario and closed after each scenario. Create a `Hooks.java` file in the `stepdefinitions` package with the following code:

```
package com.cucumber.automation.bdt.stepDefinitions;

import java.net.MalformedURLException;

import com.cucumber.automation.utils.DriverFactory;

import cucumber.api.java.After;
import cucumber.api.java.Before;

public class Hooks {

  DriverFactory df = new DriverFactory();

  @Before
    public void beforeScenario() throws
    MalformedURLException, InterruptedException{

    df.createDriver();
    }

  @After
    public void afterScenario(){
    df.teardown();
    }
}
```

14. Now we will implement **Page Object Model** (**POM**) so that maintaining and extending the Selenium code will be fairly simple. I am also keeping the POM simple; you are free to extend it in your projects.

    We will add the `page` object for the GitHub login page in the `web.pages` package and the code will look like this:

```
package com.cucumber.automation.web.pages;

import static org.junit.Assert.assertEquals;

import org.openqa.selenium.By;
import org.openqa.selenium.support.ui.ExpectedConditions;

import com.cucumber.automation.utils.DriverFactory;

public class LoginPage extends DriverFactory {

    /**
     * All locators will be mentioned here
     *
     * For this example i am not using properties file for
       reading locators
     */

    By SigninLink = By.linkText("Sign in");
    By marketingSection = By.className("marketing-section-
      signup");
    By loginSection = By.className("auth-form-body");
    By SigninButton = By.name("commit");
    By errorMessage = By.xpath("//div[@id='site-
      container']/div/div");

    /**
     * All functions related to behavior will follow now
     */
    public void ishomepageDisplayed() {
      waitVar.until(ExpectedConditions.presenceOfElementLocated
        (SigninLink));

      driver.findElement(SigninLink).isDisplayed();
      driver.findElement(marketingSection).isDisplayed();
    }

    public void clickSigninLink() {
      driver.findElement(SigninLink).click();
```

```
}

public void isloginsectionDisplayed() {
  waitVar.until(ExpectedConditions.presenceOfElementLocated
    (loginSection));
  waitVar.until(ExpectedConditions.presenceOfElementLocated
    (SigninButton));
}

public void clickSigninButton() {
  driver.findElement(SigninButton).click();
}

public void verifyErrorMessage(String msg) {
  waitVar.until(ExpectedConditions.presenceOfElementLocated
    (errorMessage));

  assertEquals(msg,
    driver.findElement(errorMessage).getText());
}
}
```

15. We will have to update the Step Definition files for the Selenium functions that we have just written. After adding all the functions, the code should look like this:

```
package com.cucumber.automation.bdt.stepDefinitions;

import com.cucumber.automation.web.pages.LoginPage;

import cucumber.api.java.en.Given;
import cucumber.api.java.en.Then;
import cucumber.api.java.en.When;

public class GithubLoginSD {

  LoginPage lp = new LoginPage();

  @Given("^user is on github homepage$")
  public void user_is_on_github_homepage() {
    lp.ishomepageDisplayed();
  }

  @When("^user clicks on Sign in button$")
  public void user_clicks_on_Sign_in_button() {
    lp.clickSigninLink();
  }
```

```java
@Then("^user is displayed login screen$")
public void user_is_displayed_login_screen() {
    lp.isloginsectionDisplayed();
}

@When("^user clicks Sign in button$")
public void user_clicks_Sign_in_button() {
    lp.clickSigninButton();
}

@Then("^user gets an error message \"(.*?)\"$")
public void user_gets_an_error_message(String arg1) {
    lp.verifyErrorMessage(arg1);
}

}
```

16. Our framework is ready to be executed. We can run this framework either from Eclipse or from the command line. Let's run this from the command line using `mvn test`. The following is the output:

```
-------------------------------------------------
 T E S T S
-------------------------------------------------
Running com.cucumber.automation.bdt.cucumberOptions.RunCukeTest
Feature: login Page
  In order to test login page
  As a Registered user
  I want to specify the login conditions

  Scenario: login without username and password               # github_login.feature:6
    Given user is on github homepage                           # GithubLoginSD.user_is_on_github_homepage()
    When user clicks on Sign in button                         # GithubLoginSD.user_clicks_on_Sign_in_button()
    Then user is displayed login screen                        # GithubLoginSD.user_is_displayed_login_screen()
    When user clicks Sign in button                            # GithubLoginSD.user_clicks_Sign_in_button()
    Then user gets an error message "Incorrect username or password." # GithubLoginSD.user_gets_an_error_message(String)

1 Scenarios (1 passed)
5 Steps (5 passed)
0m32.664s

Tests run: 6, Failures: 0, Errors: 0, Skipped: 0, Time elapsed: 33.504 sec
```

## How it works...

We have integrated Cucumber, Selenium, Maven, Java and Page Objects to design our Web Automation Framework. Cucumber is for implementing BDD, so that nontechnical people can also directly contribute to the development—Selenium for web automation, Java as a programming language, and Maven as a build tool.

Page Objects is a framework design approach for maintaining and accessing components and controls spread across test Scenarios. Page Objects creates a DSL for our tests so that if something changes on the page, we don't need to change the test; we just need to update the object that represents the page.

# Building a Mobile Automation framework

**Appium** is an open source Mobile Automation tool that has made life a lot easier for testers because it supports both Android and iOS. It has extended Selenium API, so all the Selenium advantages plus the advantage of running test cases on multiple platforms makes it an obvious choice for mobile automation.

Let's learn how we can create a robust mobile automation framework using Cucumber and Appium, along with keeping maintainability and scalability in mind using the Page Object Model.

I am just giving a demo of Android app automation; the same project and framework can be used for iOS automation as well. I will also create placeholders for iOS packages for your reference, if you want to use a single framework for both Android and iOS apps.

## Getting ready

1. Download and install Appium on your system and for more information, refer to `http://appium.io/downloads.html`.

2. Download and install Android SDK Manager from `http://developer.android.com/tools/help/sdk-manager.html`.

3. Download and install Android AVD Manager from `http://developer.android.com/tools/help/avd-manager.html`.

4. Create one Android virtual device to run the app. For more information, refer to `http://developer.android.com/tools/devices/managing-avds.html`.

Running Android on Windows or running test cases on Appium is out of the scope of this book. Readers are expected to have basic mobile automation knowledge. We will focus on creating the Cucumber Appium framework.

## How to do it...

Let's first understand the test case that we will use in this framework. We will use Agile NCR app for Android for this recipe. Let me walk-through the test Steps:

1. We open the **Agile NCR** app and verify the home page:

2. We click on the **AGENDA** option and verify the **AGENDA** screen:

3. We click on the Back button and verify the home page.

 I have included this application in the project that can be found on GitHub.

4. We are going to create a simple Maven project using the Eclipse Maven plugin. Use the same steps mentioned in first recipe to create the project and name it `CucumberMobileAutomation`.

5. Since it is a Maven project, we will update the `pom.xml` file to add the dependencies of Cucumber and Appium. As of now, this is what the `pom.xml` file looks like:

```
<project xmlns="http://maven.apache.org/POM/4.0.0"
  xmlns:xsi="http://www.w3.org/2001/XMLSchema-instance"
    xsi:schemaLocation="http://maven.apache.org/POM/4.0.0
      http://maven.apache.org/xsd/maven-4.0.0.xsd">
  <modelVersion>4.0.0</modelVersion>
  <groupId>CucumberMobileAutomation</groupId>
  <artifactId>CucumberMobileAutomation</artifactId>
  <version>0.0.1-SNAPSHOT</version>
  <name>CucumberMobileAutomation</name>
  <description>Cucumber+Appium project</description>

</project>
```

6. We will add the `properties` tag and define the properties for the Cucumber and Appium versions, so that when we need to update the dependency version, we will need to do it only at one place. Add the following code to `pom.xml`:

```
<properties>
  <appium.version>2.2.0</appium.version>
  <cucumber.version>1.2.2</cucumber.version>
</properties>
```

 To check the latest dependency version on Maven central repository, refer to `http://search.maven.org/`.

7. We will add dependency for Cucumber-JVM for BDD and Appium-Java for mobile automation. Add the following code to `pom.xml`:

```
<dependencies>
  <!-- cucumber -->
  <dependency>
    <groupId>info.cukes</groupId>
    <artifactId>cucumber-java</artifactId>
```

```
        <version>${cucumber.version}</version>
        <scope>test</scope>
    </dependency>
    <dependency>
        <groupId>info.cukes</groupId>
        <artifactId>cucumber-junit</artifactId>
        <version>${cucumber.version}</version>
        <scope>test</scope>
    </dependency>

    <!-- Appium -->
    <dependency>
        <groupId>io.appium</groupId>
        <artifactId>java-client</artifactId>
        <version>${appium.version}</version>
    </dependency>
</dependencies>
```

8. We will create the project structure and keep similar files in the same package. I am going to use the packages added for Android, and use the packages added for iOS are for reference purpose. Follow the steps shown in this screenshot and create the packages as mentioned:

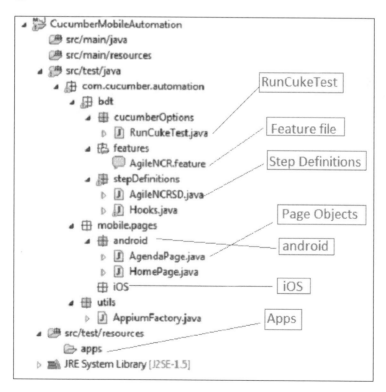

9. Since it is a Cucumber project, we are going to add the `RunCukeTest.java` file to specify the configuration, such as the location of Feature files, location of step definitions, and output location, and so on. Add the following class to the `CucumberOptions` package:

```
package com.cucumber.automation.bdt.cucumberOptions;

import org.junit.runner.RunWith;

import cucumber.api.CucumberOptions;
import cucumber.api.junit.Cucumber;

@RunWith(Cucumber.class)
@CucumberOptions(

    features =
      "src/test/java/com/cucumber/automation/bdt/features",
        glue = "com.cucumber.automation.bdt.stepDefinitions",
          plugin = {
            "pretty",
              "html:target/cucumber",
          }
)
public class RunCukeTest {
}
```

10. Now it's time to add a feature file to specify the requirements. We will add the `agile_ncr.feature` file to the package features. This is how our feature file look likes:

```
Feature: Agile NCR App
    In order to look at Agile NCR Conference
    As a Registered user
    I want to specify the flow to Agenda and Speakers

Scenario: Agenda
    Given user is on AgileNCR Home Page
    Then user gets an option Agenda
    When user selects Agenda
    Then user is on Agenda Screen
    When user chooses to go back
    Then user is on AgileNCR Home Page
```

11. The next step is to add Step Definitions. The simplest way would be to run the project once and use the suggestions given by Cucumber. Add the file `AgileNCRSD.java` to the `stepDefinitions` package, and it should contain the following code:

```java
package com.cucumber.automation.bdt.stepDefinitions;

import cucumber.api.java.en.Given;
import cucumber.api.java.en.Then;
import cucumber.api.java.en.When;

public class AgileNCRSD {


    @Given("^user is on AgileNCR Home Page$")
    public void user_is_on_AgileNCR_Home_Page()  {

    }

    @Then("^user gets an option Agenda$")
    public void user_gets_an_option_Agenda()  {

    }

    @When("^user selects Agenda$")
    public void user_selects_Agenda()  {

    }

    @Then("^user is on Agenda Screen$")
    public void user_is_on_Agenda_Screen()  {

    }

    @When("^user chooses to go back$")
    public void user_chooses_to_go_back()  {

    }

}
```

12. Now, add the `.apk` file needed to run the `app` to the apps folder in `src/test/resources`.

13. Then, we need to add the Appium functions, which can be used to invoke the Android app and close the app once the execution finishes. I am keeping this file very basic for simplicity purposes. Create the `AppiumFactory.java` class in the `utils` package and the code should look like this:

```java
package com.cucumber.automation.utils;

import io.appium.java_client.android.AndroidDriver;

import java.io.File;
import java.net.MalformedURLException;
import java.net.URL;

import org.openqa.selenium.remote.DesiredCapabilities;
import org.openqa.selenium.support.ui.WebDriverWait;

public class AppiumFactory {

  public static AndroidDriver driver = null;
  public static WebDriverWait waitVar = null;

  /**
   * This function is to invoke Appium
   *
   * @throws MalformedURLException
   * @throws InterruptedException
   */
  public void createDriver() throws MalformedURLException {

    // set up appium
    final File classpathRoot = new
      File(System.getProperty("user.dir"));
    final File appDir = new File(classpathRoot,
      "src/test/resources/apps");
    final File app = new File(appDir,
      "com.xebia.eventsapp_2.1.apk");

    final DesiredCapabilities capabilities = new
      DesiredCapabilities();
    capabilities.setCapability("platformName", "Android");
    capabilities.setCapability("deviceName", "Android
      Emulator");
    capabilities.setCapability("platformVersion", "4.4");
    capabilities.setCapability("app",
      app.getAbsolutePath());
```

```
    driver = new AndroidDriver(new
      URL("http://127.0.0.1:4723/wd/hub"),
    capabilities);

    waitVar = new WebDriverWait(driver, 90);

  }

  /**
   * This function is to close driver instance
   */
  public void teardown() {
    driver.quit();
  }
}
```

14. Now, we need to hook this code so that the browser can be initiated before each scenario and closed after each scenario. Create a `Hooks.java` file in the `stepdefinitions` package with the following code:

```java
package com.cucumber.automation.bdt.stepDefinitions;

import java.net.MalformedURLException;
import com.cucumber.automation.utils.AppiumFactory;
import cucumber.api.java.After;
import cucumber.api.java.Before;

public class Hooks {

  AppiumFactory df = new AppiumFactory();

  @Before
  public void beforeScenario() throws
    MalformedURLException, InterruptedException{
    df.createDriver();
  }

  @After
  public void afterScenario(){
    df.teardown();
  }
}
```

15. Now, we will implement the POM, so that maintaining and extending Appium code will be fairly simple. I am also keeping the POM simple; you are free to extend it in your projects.

We will add two page objects, one for `HomePage` and the other for `AgendaPage`. The code for `HomePage.java` looks like this:

```
package com.cucumber.automation.mobile.pages.android;

import static org.junit.Assert.assertTrue;
import org.openqa.selenium.By;
import org.openqa.selenium.support.ui.ExpectedConditions;
import com.cucumber.automation.utils.AppiumFactory;

public class HomePage extends AppiumFactory {

  /**
   * All locators will be mentioned here
   *
   * For this example i am not using properties file for
     reading locators
   */
  By homePageImage = By.id
    ("com.xebia.eventsapp:id/home_banner_imageView");
  By agendaButton = By.id
    ("com.xebia.eventsapp:id/home_agenda_title");


  By backButton = By.id("android:id/home");


  /**
   * All functions related to behavior will follow now
   */
  public void verifyHomePage(){
    waitVar.until
      (ExpectedConditions.presenceOfElementLocated
        (homePageImage));
    assertTrue
      (driver.findElement(homePageImage).isDisplayed());
  }

  public void verifyHomePageOptions(){
    waitVar.until
      (ExpectedConditions.presenceOfElementLocated
        (homePageImage));
```

```
      waitVar.until
        (ExpectedConditions.elementToBeClickable
          (agendaButton));

      assertTrue
        (driver.findElement(agendaButton).isDisplayed());
  }

  public void clickAgenda(){
    driver.findElement(agendaButton).click();
  }
}
```

The code for `AgendaPage.java` looks like this:

```
package com.cucumber.automation.mobile.pages.android;

import static org.junit.Assert.*;
import org.openqa.selenium.By;
import org.openqa.selenium.support.ui.ExpectedConditions;
import com.cucumber.automation.utils.AppiumFactory;

public class AgendaPage extends AppiumFactory {

  // All the locators for Agenda page will be defined here
  By title = By.id
    ("com.xebia.eventsapp:id/action_bar_custom_title");
  By AgendaList = By.className
    ("android.widget.LinearLayout");

  By backButton = By.id("android:id/home");

  // All the behavior of Agenda page will be defined here
    in functions
  public void verifyAgendaPage() {

    waitVar.until
      (ExpectedConditions.presenceOfElementLocated(title));

    assertEquals("Agenda",
      driver.findElement(title).getText());
    assertTrue
      (driver.findElements(AgendaList).size() >= 0);
  }

  public void clickBack() {
```

```
      driver.findElement(backButton).click();
   }

}
```

16. We will have to update the Step Definition files for the Selenium functions that we have just written. After adding all the functions, the code should look like this:

```java
package com.cucumber.automation.bdt.stepDefinitions;

import com.cucumber.automation.mobile.pages.android.AgendaPage;
import com.cucumber.automation.mobile.pages.android.HomePage;

import cucumber.api.java.en.Given;
import cucumber.api.java.en.Then;
import cucumber.api.java.en.When;

public class AgileNCRSD {

  HomePage hp = new HomePage();
  AgendaPage ap = new AgendaPage();

  @Given("^user is on AgileNCR Home Page$")
  public void user_is_on_AgileNCR_Home_Page() {
    hp.verifyHomePage();
  }

  @Then("^user gets an option Agenda$")
  public void user_gets_an_option_Agenda() {
    hp.verifyHomePageOptions();
  }

  @When("^user selects Agenda$")
  public void user_selects_Agenda() {
    hp.clickAgenda();
  }

  @Then("^user is on Agenda Screen$")
  public void user_is_on_Agenda_Screen() {
    ap.verifyAgendaPage();
  }

  @When("^user chooses to go back$")
  public void user_chooses_to_go_back() {
    ap.clickBack();
  }

}
```

17. Our framework is ready. Before we can start the execution, we need to start the Appium server. Start the Appium server with the default settings, as shown in the following screenshot:

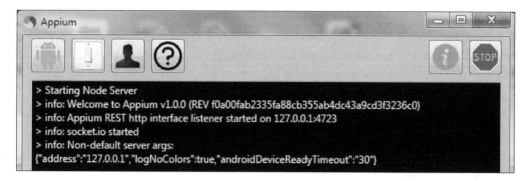

18. We can run this framework either from Eclipse or from the command line. Let's run this from the command line using `mvn test`. The following is the output:

```
--------------------------------------------------------
 T E S T S
--------------------------------------------------------
Running com.cucumber.automation.bdt.cucumberOptions.RunCukeTest
Feature: Agile NCR App
  In order to look at Agile NCR Conference
  As a Registered user
  I want to specify the flow to Agenda and Speakers

  Scenario: Agenda                         # AgileNCR.feature:6
    Given user is on AgileNCR Home Page    # AgileNCRSD.user_is_on_AgileNCR_Home_Page()
    Then user gets an option Agenda        # AgileNCRSD.user_gets_an_option_Agenda()
    When user selects Agenda               # AgileNCRSD.user_selects_Agenda()
    Then user is on Agenda Screen          # AgileNCRSD.user_is_on_Agenda_Screen()
    When user chooses to go back           # AgileNCRSD.user_chooses_to_go_back()
    Then user is on AgileNCR Home Page     # AgileNCRSD.user_is_on_AgileNCR_Home_Page()

1 Scenarios (1 passed)
6 Steps (6 passed)
1m36.165s

Tests run: 7, Failures: 0, Errors: 0, Skipped: 0, Time elapsed: 96.913 sec

Results :

Tests run: 7, Failures: 0, Errors: 0, Skipped: 0
```

## How it works...

We have integrated Cucumber, Appium, Maven, Java, and Page Objects to design our Mobile Automation framework. Cucumber is for implementing BDD, so that nontechnical people can also directly contribute to the development—Appium for web automation, Java as a programming language, and Maven as a build tool.

Page Objects is a framework design approach for maintaining and accessing components and controls spread across test Scenarios. Page Object creates a DSL for our tests; thus, if something changes on the page, we don't need to change the test; we just need to update the object that represents the page.

# Building a REST Automation framework

HTTP Client is an open source REST services library developed by Apache. I am using HTTP Client for this framework because this is a pure Java implementation and is very easy to use. We need to create an instance of the HTTP client and then just use one of the already defined functions.

Since there is no UI involved and there is a limit to the functions that we need to use, there is no need for the POM in this framework. Let's learn how we can create a robust REST automation framework using Cucumber and HTTP Client.

 I am just giving a demo of REST Services automation, the same project and framework can be used for SOAP automation as well.

## How to do it...

Let's first understand the test case that we will use in this framework. I am going to test the GET and POST methods. Let me walk-through the test Steps.

1. Send a GET request to the GitHub URL at https://api.github.com/users/ShankarGarg to verify the user details.

2. Send a POST request to the Apple service center at https://selfsolve.apple.com/wcResults.do to register your device.

3. We are going to create a simple Maven project using the Eclipse Maven plugin. Use the same steps mentioned in first recipe to create the project and name it CucumberRESTAutomation.

4. Since it is a Maven project, we will update the pom.xml file for adding dependencies of Cucumber and Appium. As of now, this is how the pom.xml file looks like:

```
<project xmlns="http://maven.apache.org/POM/4.0.0"
  xmlns:xsi="http://www.w3.org/2001/XMLSchema-instance"
    xsi:schemaLocation="http://maven.apache.org/POM/4.0.0
      http://maven.apache.org/xsd/maven-4.0.0.xsd">
  <modelVersion>4.0.0</modelVersion>
  <groupId>CucumberRESTAutomation</groupId>
  <artifactId>CucumberRESTAutomation</artifactId>
  <version>0.0.1-SNAPSHOT</version>
```

```
    <name>CucumberRESTAutomation</name>
    <description>Cucumber+HTTP Client project</description>
</project>
```

5. We will add the `properties` tag and define the properties for the Cucumber and Appium versions, so that when we need to update the dependency version we will need to do it only at one place. Add the following code to `pom.xml`:

```
<properties>
  <http.version>4.4.1</http.version>
  <cucumber.version>1.2.2</cucumber.version>
</properties>
```

 To check the latest dependency version on Maven central repository, refer to `http://search.maven.org/`.

6. We will add dependency for Cucumber-JVM for BDD, Appium-java for mobile automation. Add the following code to `pom.xml`:

```
<dependencies>
  <!-- cucumber -->
  <dependency>
    <groupId>info.cukes</groupId>
    <artifactId>cucumber-java</artifactId>
    <version>${cucumber.version}</version>
    <scope>test</scope>
  </dependency>
  <dependency>
    <groupId>info.cukes</groupId>
    <artifactId>cucumber-junit</artifactId>
    <version>${cucumber.version}</version>
    <scope>test</scope>
  </dependency>

  <!-- HTTPClient -->
  <dependency>
    <groupId>org.apache.httpcomponents</groupId>
    <artifactId>httpclient</artifactId>
    <version>${http.version}</version>
  </dependency>
</dependencies>
```

7. We will create the project structure and will keep similar files in the same package. Follow the steps shown in this screenshot and create the packages as mentioned:

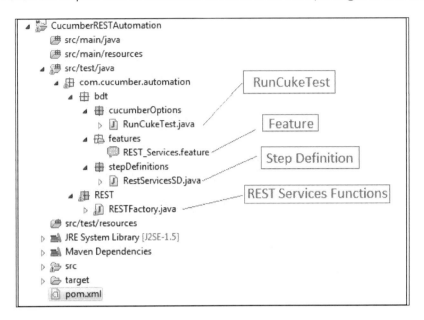

8. Since it is a Cucumber project, we are going to add the `RunCukeTest.java` file to specify the configuration, such as the location of feature files, the location of step definitions, the output location, and so on. Add the following class to the `CucumberOptions` package:

```
package com.cucumber.automation.bdt.cucumberOptions;

import org.junit.runner.RunWith;

import cucumber.api.CucumberOptions;
import cucumber.api.junit.Cucumber;

@RunWith(Cucumber.class)
@CucumberOptions(

   features =
     "src/test/java/com/cucumber/automation/bdt/features",
   glue = "com.cucumber.automation.bdt.stepDefinitions",
   plugin = {
     "pretty",
       "html:target/cucumber",
   }
)
public class RunCukeTest {
}
```

9. Now it's time to add the feature file to specify the requirements. We will add the `REST_Services.feature` file to the package features. This is how our feature file look likes:

```
Feature: SOA Test
  In order to test rest services
  As a Registered user
  I want to specify the rest services test conditions

  Scenario: GET Request - GIT Hub User details
    When user sends a GET request with "https://api.github.com/
users/ShankarGarg"
    Then status code should be 200
    And response type should be "json"
    And response contains user name "Shankar Garg"

  Scenario: POST Request - Register a user
    When user sends a POST request to
        "https://selfsolve.apple.com/wcResults.do" with
         following details
         | key    | value       |
         | sn     | C2WGC14ADRJ7 |
         | cn     |             |
         | locale |             |
         | caller |             |
         | num    | 12345       |
    Then status code should be 200
    And response type should be "html"
    And response contains user name "C2WGC14ADRJ7"
```

10. The next step is to add Step Definitions. The simplest way would be run the project once and use the suggestions given by Cucumber. Add a `RESTServicesSD.java` file to the `stepDefinitions` package and it should have the following code:

```
package com.cucumber.automation.bdt.stepDefinitions;

import cucumber.api.DataTable;
import cucumber.api.java.en.Then;
import cucumber.api.java.en.When;

public class RestServicesSD {

  @When("^user sends a GET request with \"(.*?)\"$")
  public void user_sends_a_GET_request_with(String arg1) {
  }
```

```
@Then("^status code should be (\\d+)$")
public void status_code_should_be(int arg1) {
}


@Then("^response type should be \"(.*?)\"$")
public void response_type_should_be(String arg1) {
}


@Then("^response contains user name \"(.*?)\"$")
public void response_contains_user_name(String arg1) {
}


@When("^user sends a POST request to \"(.*?)\" with
  follwoing details$")
public void
  user_sends_a_POST_request_to_with_follwoing_details(
    String arg1, DataTable arg2) {
  }


}
```

11. Now we need to add the HTTP Client functions, which can be used to send the
    GET and POST methods. For demonstration purposes, I am keeping the minimum
    required functions in the file.

```
package com.cucumber.automation.REST;

import static org.junit.Assert.*;

import java.io.IOException;
import java.util.ArrayList;
import java.util.List;

import org.apache.http.HttpEntity;
import org.apache.http.HttpResponse;
import org.apache.http.NameValuePair;
import org.apache.http.ParseException;
import org.apache.http.client.ClientProtocolException;
import org.apache.http.client.HttpClient;
import org.apache.http.client.config.RequestConfig;
import org.apache.http.client.entity.UrlEncodedFormEntity;
import org.apache.http.client.methods.HttpGet;
import org.apache.http.client.methods.HttpPost;
```

```java
import org.apache.http.client.methods.HttpUriRequest;
import org.apache.http.entity.ContentType;
import org.apache.http.impl.client.DefaultHttpClient;
import org.apache.http.impl.client.HttpClientBuilder;
import org.apache.http.message.BasicNameValuePair;
import org.apache.http.util.EntityUtils;

import cucumber.api.DataTable;

public class RESTFactory {

  @SuppressWarnings("deprecation")
  HttpClient client = new DefaultHttpClient();
  static HttpResponse httpResponse = null;
  static String responseString = null;
  String getURL = "";

  public void getRequest(String url) throws
    ClientProtocolException, IOException{
    RequestConfig requestConfig =
      RequestConfig.custom().setConnectionRequestTimeout
        (20000).setConnectTimeout(20000).setSocketTimeout
          (20000).build();
    HttpClientBuilder builder =
      HttpClientBuilder.create().setDefaultRequestConfig
        (requestConfig);
    getURL = url;
    HttpUriRequest request = new HttpGet( url );

    httpResponse = builder.build().execute( request );

  }

  public void verifyStatusCode(int statusCode) throws
    ClientProtocolException, IOException {
    assertEquals(statusCode,
      httpResponse.getStatusLine().getStatusCode());
  }

  public void verifyResponseType(String type){
    String mimeType =
      ContentType.getOrDefault
        (httpResponse.getEntity()).getMimeType();
    assertTrue( mimeType.contains(type) );
```

```
    }

    public void verifyResponseData(String responseData)
      throws ParseException, IOException{
      HttpEntity entity = httpResponse.getEntity();
      responseString = EntityUtils.toString(entity, "UTF-8");

      assertTrue(responseString.contains(responseData));
    }

    public void postRequest
      (String url, DataTable payloadTable)
        throws ClientProtocolException, IOException{
      List<List<String>> payload = payloadTable.raw();

      HttpPost post = new HttpPost(url);
      List<NameValuePair> urlParameters = new
        ArrayList<NameValuePair>(1);

      for (int i=1; i<payload.size();i++){
        urlParameters.add(new
          BasicNameValuePair(payload.get(i).get(0),
            payload.get(i).get(1)));
      }

      post.setEntity(new
        UrlEncodedFormEntity(urlParameters));

      httpResponse = client.execute(post);
    }
  }
```

 Readers are expected to know the basics about REST Services—the different functions such as GET and POST methods.

12. We don't need any hooks files here because we don't need to invoke any browsers/ apps before or after the test cases. If need be, we can always add the file later.

13. We don't need the Page Object Model here because there are no UI pages that we need to maintain.

14. We will have to update the Step Definition files for the HTTP functions that we have just written. After adding all the functions, the code should look like this:

```java
package com.cucumber.automation.bdt.stepDefinitions;

import java.io.IOException;

import org.apache.http.ParseException;
import org.apache.http.client.ClientProtocolException;

import com.cucumber.automation.REST.RESTFactory;

import cucumber.api.DataTable;
import cucumber.api.java.en.Then;
import cucumber.api.java.en.When;

public class RestServicesSD {

  RESTFactory rt = new RESTFactory();

  @When("^user sends a GET request with \"(.*?)\"$")
  public void user_sends_a_GET_request_with(String url)
    throws ClientProtocolException, IOException {
      rt.getRequest(url);
  }

  @Then("^status code should be (\\d+)$")
  public void status_code_should_be(int statuscode) throws
    ClientProtocolException, IOException {
      rt.verifyStatusCode(statuscode);
  }

  @Then("^response type should be \"(.*?)\"$")
  public void response_type_should_be(String type) {
      rt.verifyResponseType(type);
  }

  @Then("^response contains user name \"(.*?)\"$")
  public void response_contains_user_name(String userName)
    throws ParseException, IOException {
      rt.verifyResponseData(userName);
  }

  @When("^user sends a POST request to \"(.*?)\" with
    follwoing details$")
```

```
    public void
      user_sends_a_POST_request_to_with_follwoing_details
        (String url, DataTable payload) throws
          ClientProtocolException, IOException {
      rt.postRequest(url, payload);
    }
  }
}
```

15. Our framework is ready and we can run this framework from either Eclipse or the Terminal. Let's run this from the command line using `mvn test`. The following is the output:

```
T E S T S
-------------------------------------------------
Running com.cucumber.automation.bdt.cucumberOptions.RunCukeTest
Feature: SOA Test
  In order to test rest services
  As a Registered user
  I want to specify the rest services test conditions

  Scenario: GET Request - GIT Hub User details                                              # REST_Services.feature:6
    When user sends a GET request with "https://api.github.com/users/ShankarGarg" # RestServicesSD.user_sends_a_GET_request_with(String)
    Then status code should be 200                                                # RestServicesSD.status_code_should_be(int)
    And response type should be "json"                                            # RestServicesSD.response_type_should_be(String)
    And response contains user name "Shankar Garg"                                # RestServicesSD.response_contains_user_name(String)

  Scenario: POST Request - Register a user                                                   # REST_Services.feature:12
    When user sends a POST request to "https://selfsolve.apple.com/wcResults.do" with follwoing details # RestServicesSD.user_sends_a_POST_request_to_with_fo
llows(String,DataTable)
    Then status code should be 200                                                # RestServicesSD.status_code_should_be(int)
    And response type should be "html"                                            # RestServicesSD.response_type_should_be(String)
    And response contains user name "C2WGC14ADRJ7"                                # RestServicesSD.response_contains_user_name(String)

2 Scenarios (2 passed)
8 Steps (8 passed)
0m3.976s

Tests run: 10, Failures: 0, Errors: 0, Skipped: 0, Time elapsed: 4.646 sec
```

## How it works...

We have integrated Cucumber, HTTP Client, Maven, Java and Page Objects to design our REST Services automation framework. Cucumber is for implementing BDD, so that nontechnical people can also directly contribute to the development—HTTP Client for REST automation, Java as a programming language, and Maven as a build tool.

# Index

## Symbols

## A

## B

## C

## Console output

## D

transforming, to parse test data 36-39

**Doc Strings**
and Scenario Outlines, combining 43, 44
used, for parsing big data as one
chunk 41, 42

**dryRun option**
about 69
working 70

**Duplicate Step Definitions**
identifying 28-31

# E

**Eclipse**
Maven project import, URL 84

# F

**Feature files**
about 1
backgrounds, adding 8-11
creating, in native languages 17, 18
independent Scenario, benefits 7
issues 9
Scenarios 3
Steps 3
with multiple Scenarios, writing 6, 7
with one Scenario, writing 2, 3
**fixtures 47**

# G

**GET request**
sending, URL 128
**GitHub**
Cucumber, integrating with 90-94
URL 90, 104

# H

**Hooks**
about 57
adding, to Cucumber code 55-58
After Hook 57
Before Hook 57
NOTing 64
tagging 58-60
**HTML 78**

# I

**issues, Feature files**
duplication 9
maintainability 9
readability 9
repetition 9

# J

**Jenkins**
Cucumber, integrating with 90-94
URL 90
**JSON 79**
**JUnit**
about 80
Cucumber, integrating with 65, 66

# K

**keywords 2**

# M

**Maven**
Cucumber, integrating with 83-85
for Mac, URL 84
for Windows, URL 84
**Maven central repository**
URL 108, 118, 129
**Mobile Automation framework**
building 116-127
**monochrome option 72**
**multiple arguments**
sending, in Steps 11, 12

# N

**naming conventions**
configuring 80, 81
**Noncapture Group**
using 34-36

# O

**Optional Capture**
using 34-36
**options, Cucumber**
Features 68

Glue  68
overriding  67, 68
Tags  68

**ORing**
Hooks  64
tagged Hooks  60-64
Tags  5

# P

**Page Object Model (POM)  113**
**POST request**
sending, URL  128

# R

**regular expressions**
used, for optimizing Step Definitions  32-34
**REST Automation framework**
building  128-135

# S

**Scenario Outlines**
and Doc Strings, combining  43, 44
combining, with backgrounds  18-20
combining, with Scenarios  18-20
implementing  14,-16
**Scenarios**
combining, with backgrounds  18-20
combining, with Scenario Outlines  18-20
creating, with And keyword  4, 5
creating, with But keyword  4, 5
expected output  3
Given  4
pre-condition  3
Then  4
user action  3
When  4
**Scenario Title  3**
**Selenium**
about  104
URL  104
**Snippets option  81**

**Step Definitions**
creating  22-26
implemented Steps  27
optimizing, with regular expressions  32-34
pending Steps  27
Steps  27
Undefined Steps  27
**strict option**
working  70, 71
**String transformations**
defining  45, 46

# T

**tables**
comparing, for Data Table
implementation  39-41
**tagged Hooks**
ANDing  60-64
ORing  60-64
**Tags**
about  48
ANDing  51-55
ORing  51-55
using  48-50
working  50, 51
**Terminal**
Cucumber, running from  85-87
options, overriding  88-90
**test cases**
running, in parallel  94-101
**test data**
parsing, for Data Table transformation  36-39

# W

**Web Automation framework**
building  104-115

# Thank you for buying
# Cucumber Cookbook

## About Packt Publishing

Packt, pronounced 'packed', published its first book, *Mastering phpMyAdmin for Effective MySQL Management*, in April 2004, and subsequently continued to specialize in publishing highly focused books on specific technologies and solutions.

Our books and publications share the experiences of your fellow IT professionals in adapting and customizing today's systems, applications, and frameworks. Our solution-based books give you the knowledge and power to customize the software and technologies you're using to get the job done. Packt books are more specific and less general than the IT books you have seen in the past. Our unique business model allows us to bring you more focused information, giving you more of what you need to know, and less of what you don't.

Packt is a modern yet unique publishing company that focuses on producing quality, cutting-edge books for communities of developers, administrators, and newbies alike. For more information, please visit our website at www.packtpub.com.

## About Packt Open Source

In 2010, Packt launched two new brands, Packt Open Source and Packt Enterprise, in order to continue its focus on specialization. This book is part of the Packt open source brand, home to books published on software built around open source licenses, and offering information to anybody from advanced developers to budding web designers. The Open Source brand also runs Packt's open source Royalty Scheme, by which Packt gives a royalty to each open source project about whose software a book is sold.

## Writing for Packt

We welcome all inquiries from people who are interested in authoring. Book proposals should be sent to author@packtpub.com. If your book idea is still at an early stage and you would like to discuss it first before writing a formal book proposal, then please contact us; one of our commissioning editors will get in touch with you.

We're not just looking for published authors; if you have strong technical skills but no writing experience, our experienced editors can help you develop a writing career, or simply get some additional reward for your expertise.

## Instant Cucumber BDD
## How-to

ISBN: 978-1-78216-348-0 Paperback: 70 pages

A short and quick guide to mastering behavior-driven software development with Cucumber

1. Learn something new in an Instant! A short, fast, focused guide delivering immediate results.

2. A step-by-step process of developing a real project in a BDD-style using Cucumber.

3. Pro tips for writing Cucumber features and steps.

## Learning Behavior-driven
## Development with JavaScript

ISBN: 978-1-78439-264-2 Paperback: 392 pages

Create powerful yet simple-to-code BDD test suites in JavaScript using the most popular tools in the community

1. Master the most popular testing tools in the JavaScript ecosystem, such as CucumberJS, Mocha, SinonJS, and more.

2. Learn how Behavior-driven development can help you to write software that is more modular and has less defects.

3. Avoid common mistakes in testing, simplify your test suites, and make them more maintainable using a very pragmatic approach to BDD.

Please check **www.PacktPub.com** for information on our titles

## Test-Driven Development with Mockito

ISBN: 978-1-78328-329-3          Paperback: 172 pages

Learn how to apply Test-Driven Development and the Mockito framework in real life projects, using realistic, hands-on examples

1. Start writing clean, high quality code to apply Design Patterns and principles.

2. Add new features to your project by applying Test-first development- JUnit 4.0 and Mockito framework.

3. Make legacy code testable and clean up technical debts.

## Ruby on Rails Web Mashup Projects

ISBN: 978-1-84719-393-3          Paperback: 272 pages

A step-by-step tutorial to building web mashups

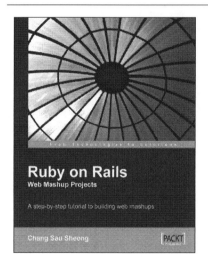

1. Learn about web mashup applications and mashup plug-ins.

2. Create practical real-life web mashup projects step by step.

3. Access and mash up many different APIs with Ruby and Ruby on Rails.

Please check **www.PacktPub.com** for information on our titles

Made in the USA
Middletown, DE
02 April 2019